"Kwek Leng Beng's story is worth reading. In my years interacting with him as a government minister and as a friend, I found him thoughtful, realistic and creative. He is not given to publicity or flashy living. He is a worrier. His lifework consisted of building on what he inherited from his father and turning CDL into a remarkable international enterprise."

~ **George Yeo**, *former Cabinet Minister of Singapore*

"I have known LB in the same industry for 35 years and there are very few people who have weathered the significant ups and downs of the hotel business better than him. I have admired his tenacity, instincts and pure determination at building CDL into the organisation it is today — an amazing achievement by an amazing man and it is my pleasure to call him my friend."

~ **Sir David Michels**, *former Chief Executive of the Hilton Group and former President of the British Hospitality Association*

"The fascinating story of one of Singapore's great entrepreneurs and developers. The mysterious Kwek Leng Beng comes to life as he travels the world and builds a great hotel empire, real estate developments and a wide variety of other businesses. His insight and determination saved the Marina Bay Sands' design and enabled its realisation. This is a tale of power, wealth, combined with sheer determination, which reads as a metaphor for Singapore's rise as a nation."

~ **Moshe Safdie**, *architect of Marina Bay Sands and Jewel Changi Airport*

"Kwek Leng Beng is a maverick entrepreneur who is deeply passionate about hotels and properties. He has put Singapore on the map with his hotels around the world. There are few Asian business leaders with his proven track record across six decades. *Strictly Business* tells you the secrets behind this master dealmaker's success."

~ **Philip Yeo**, *former Chairman of the Economic Development Board in Singapore*

"Over my two-decades-long relationship, I have found Chairman Kwek smart, practical, honest, and loyal to his friends. I admire and respect him not only as a professional business person but also as a personal friend. He is a man of his word. I think very highly of him. This long overdue book captures his sharp business instincts. It places him among the giants of Asia's top business leaders."

~ **W. Chan Kim**, *Distinguished Professor and Co-director of the INSEAD Blue Ocean Strategy Institute, named the Most Influential Management Thinker in the world*

"I have been privileged to know Chairman Kwek Leng Beng since the early days of Hong Leong Group, CDL, and Millennium & Copthorne Hotels. I have watched with admiration how he has built these companies into highly successful property and hotel owners, internationally as well as in Singapore. He is one of the world's great business leaders. Managing different businesses in different countries is complicated and few people have this skill set, but Chairman Kwek clearly does. Chairman Kwek has received numerous awards for his business acumen and for his ability to succeed in diverse sectors — property, hotels and finance — around the world. His is one of the great international success stories, so his book will be a compelling read."

~ **Sir John Bond**, *former Chairman of HSBC*

STRICTLY BUSINESS

THE
KWEK LENG BENG
STORY

STRICTLY BUSINESS

THE
KWEK LENG BENG
STORY

PEH SHING HUEI
Winner of the Singapore Literature Prize

World Scientific

THE NUTGRAF BOOKS

Published by

World Scientific Publishing Co. Pte. Ltd.
5 Toh Tuck Link, Singapore 596224
USA office: 27 Warren Street, Suite 401-402, Hackensack, NJ 07601
UK office: 57 Shelton Street, Covent Garden, London WC2H 9HE

and

The Nutgraf Holdings Pte Ltd
18 Howard Road, Novelty BizCentre #06-06, Singapore 369585

National Library Board, Singapore Cataloguing in Publication Data
Name(s): Peh, Shing Huei.
Title: Strictly business : the Kwek Leng Beng story / Peh Shing Huei.
Description: Singapore : World Scientific Publishing Co. Pte. Ltd. and
Nutgraf Holdings Pte Ltd, [2024]
Identifier(s): ISBN 978-981-12-8448-9 (hardcover) | 978-981-12-8451-9 (paperback) |
978-981-12-8449-6 (ebook for institutions) | 978-981-12-8450-2 (ebook for individuals)
Subject(s): LCSH: Kwek, Leng Beng. | Businesspeople--Singapore--Biography. |
Chinese--Singapore--Biography.
Classification: DDC 338.092--dc23

British Library Cataloguing-in-Publication Data
A catalogue record for this book is available from the British Library.

For any available supplementary material, please visit
https://www.worldscientific.com/worldscibooks/10.1142/13630#t=suppl

Desk Editors: Jiang Yulin/Ong Shi Min Nicole

Printed in Singapore

Foreword

S*trictly Business* — a simple title that so aptly encapsulates the very spirit of my business and life journey. For as long as I can remember, most of my life has been devoted to learning and doing business. It is my passion, my strength, my purpose.

Why so? I am not sure. Perhaps business talks were always part of dinner conversations growing up. Or maybe it was to prove to my late father and my family I was worth my salt. Perhaps it was the weight of personal ambition and corporate responsibilities that propelled me to pursue building a successful enterprise. Regardless of the reason, "business as usual" is my motto.

It is also for this reason I never had the time to pause and consider a biography. Despite the protestations of friends and associates over the years, there was always another business deal to close, an opportunity to seize, a work trip to take, or a growing company to manage.

However, in 2020, the COVID-19 pandemic hit globally — the world came to a standstill. Hong Leong Group, like many other businesses, was affected and we had to wait out the storm. The following year, I turned 80 and was again urged to write my memoirs. In a phase of introspection, I relented. It seemed like the right time. If not now, when? I thought.

The Hong Leong Group, founded by my late father, Kwek Hong Png in 1941, is very much part of Singapore's history. As one of Singapore's pioneers, my father helped shape and grow the country's key industries, such as real estate, construction, hotels and finance. There were neither manuscripts nor a prescribed formula — except the persistence of an entrepreneurial spirit.

I joined the Group in 1963 fresh out of university. I learnt many important business and life principles from my father and the remarkable individuals I have worked with over the decades. In 1990, when I was appointed to lead the Group as its chairman, I leaned on my experiences to guide me, read more to hone my skills, took calculated risks, followed my gut instincts, and made some difficult choices. I celebrated achievements but rolled with the punches, persevering through adversity.

Today, as I look at our cityscape, I marvel at how it has evolved and how our Group has been so much part of the Singapore Story. Through this book, I share some lessons that have guided my business thinking and shaped my philosophy through the struggles of entrepreneurship and some of its achievements. I hope it will be a source of inspiration for those aspiring to make their mark in the world of business.

Every generation will face its challenges and chart its own path.

I hope my stories will resonate, inspire and connect people across generations, cultures and geographies.

Strictly Business is not about board meetings, spreadsheets and feasibility studies; it sketches the challenges embraced and innovations worked on, and a desire to build a lasting legacy.

With Heartfelt Appreciation

For me, the real challenge was sitting down with Peh Shing Huei, the book's writer, for hours of conversations for this book. I thank him for his patience and perseverance as he and his dedicated team at The Nutgraf worked on this project. To Gerry De Silva, who heads our Group's Corporate Affairs and was lead coordinator when this project started some two years or more ago to its completion — from the initial sourcing of potential writers, planning interviews, hunting for hidden gems in archives to husbanding the workflow on photos to the book's completion.

Gerry was also part of a steering committee who read through all the manuscript versions. Like silent guardians, they offered candid views, undertook the important work of fact-checking, and gave valuable insights and perspectives of the narrative that was developing for this book. A big thank you to Shing Huei and the Steering Committee who were ably supported by the teams at The Nutgraf, Hong Leong Group Corporate Affairs and World Scientific Publishing. Thank you for the hard work put in to enable this book to see the light of day.

I am deeply grateful to the Singapore Government for its visionary leadership and foresight, which played a pivotal role in transforming our country into a thriving metropolis. The robust infrastructure, effective governance and global reputation of Singapore have contributed to the success of our Group, both locally and internationally.

To my immediate family for their enduring support, encouragement, sacrifices and understanding. You all have been a constant source of strength to me.

My dear wife Cecilia, thank you for your spontaneous wit, wise judgment, and tolerance. You have understood my obligation to continue my late father's legacy. You have been my anchor through many storms and steadfastly supported my responsibilities to achieve new heights for the Hong Leong Group. Thank you for your love and companionship on this journey.

To my sons Sherman and Kingston, you have grown to be incredible individuals professionally and personally. You are always close to my heart. I'm proud of the impact you are making in the marketplace and the love and joy you share with your own families.

To my grandchildren, you always hold a special place in my heart. Your infectious laughter brings me joy. You remind me of the beauty in simplicity, inspiring me to do better.

My heartfelt appreciation to Philip Yeo, Philip Ng, George Yeo, Professor W. Chan Kim, Sir David Michels, Sir John Bond and Moshe Safdie for their kind endorsements and sharing of anecdotes. I value the decades-long friendship that has stood the test of time.

Finally, I dedicate this book to my loved ones, who have been my unwavering support through the highs and lows, many of whom have been featured in the book.

Kwek Leng Beng

Foreword

I have known Kwek Leng Beng (whom I call LB with affection) for over 38 years and am privileged to witness the ascent of CDL over the past four decades with admiration. No one has done as much to build this world-class company with its trusted brand in Singapore. LB was the prime mover in spreading the wings of CDL into other markets with astute investments in prime real estate at opportune times in the market cycle invariably, as well as to assemble an international chain of hotels — never an easy feat as real estate success rarely transcends geographical boundaries. LB is one of the most respected personalities in Asian real estate and his biography will be a precious recollection of how the enterprise was built through the ups and downs of the property cycle as well as global business cycle, his knack for the deals be it at home or abroad, and his instinctive understanding of international real estate. It is a valuable part of the annals of Singapore real estate and business, and most certainly an essential read for those of us in business.

Philip Ng
Chief Executive Officer
Far East Organization

Timeline

1941	Jan 27: Kwek Leng Beng is born — the second of five children of Kwek Hong Png
1963	Graduates from University of London with a Bachelor of Laws; enters family business as management executive
1967	Joins Hong Leong Finance as general manager and director
1969	Buys stake in loss-making property firm City Developments Limited (CDL)
1970	Marries lawyer Cecilia Kok; opens his first hotel, King's Hotel (now known as Copthorne King's) at Havelock Road in Singapore
1972–3	Takes majority stake in CDL and management control of the company

1979	Leads Hong Leong Finance to acquire Singapore Finance, becoming Singapore's largest finance company
1984	Takes over chairmanship of Hong Leong Finance from his father
1990	Succeeds his father as chairman of Hong Leong Group
1992–4	Begins global hotel expansion with major acquisitions in London, New Zealand and New York
1995	Makes global headlines when he and Prince Alwaleed bin Talal buy the Plaza Hotel in New York from Donald Trump; Kwek follows up by buying the 16-hotel Copthorne chain in Europe
1996	Floats Millennium & Copthorne Hotels on the London Stock Exchange — the first Singapore company to do so
1997	Wins Businessman of the Year Award by *The Business Times* in Singapore
1998	Opens Republic Plaza, one of Singapore's tallest skyscrapers and the Hong Leong Group's new flagship building

1999	Buys Regal chain of 47 hotels in the United States and the Seoul Hilton in South Korea
2000	Honoured as Asia Pacific Hotelier of the Decade at the Annual Asia Pacific Hotel Industry Investment Conference for Hoteliers
2001	Singapore Prime Minister Goh Chok Tong praises Kwek as a role model businessman at the annual National Day Rally; September 11 attacks destroy the Millenium Hotel
2003	Reopens the Millenium Hilton Hotel to much fanfare after a US$32-million renovation makeover
2004	Launches The Sail, Singapore's then tallest residential building
2005–6	Enters joint venture with Las Vegas Sands to build Marina Bay Sands, but exits a month later
2014	Wins inaugural Real Estate Developers' Association of Singapore (REDAS) Lifetime Achievement Award

2016	Launches The South Beach, an iconic integrated development of hotel, residences, offices, shops and restaurants
2020–1	Sincere incident leads to a loss of S$1.8 billion, one of the biggest setbacks in Kwek's career
2021	CDL announces the sale of Millennium Hilton Seoul for US$845 million
2023	CDL celebrates 60th anniversary; Kwek and CDL donate S$24 million to the Singapore Institute of Technology to establish the Kwek Leng Beng University Tower in the school's new campus in Punggol

Contents

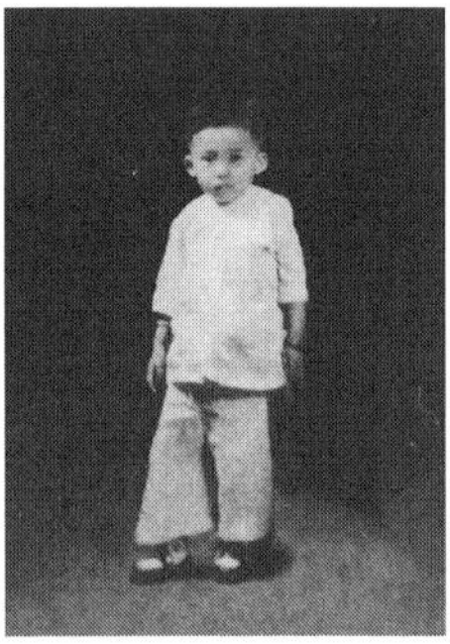

Hilton

Introduction

When architect Moshe Safdie decided to put a SkyPark with an infinity pool atop and across three hotel towers, he knew right away that it was a winning idea. "It made so much sense: a sky park, with unbelievable views to Indonesia, to Malaysia, to the downtown, to the harbour, to the sea," he wrote in his autobiography. But the developer Sheldon Adelson hated it. The boss of Las Vegas Sands wanted a design to win the bid to build an integrated resort in Singapore in 2006, and the concept of a flying ship did not appeal to him at all. "Adelson responded with colourful language and told me to take the SkyPark off, calling it a stupid idea," recalled Safdie. Adelson also thought it was too expensive: "You're out of your goddamn mind," he said. The architect refused, and threatened to walk away.

A Singaporean architect attached to Safdie in Boston, United States, panicked. He was part of the City Developments Limited (CDL) team which had partnered Sands to tender for the resort which would come to be known as Marina Bay Sands, or MBS. He called his boss Kwek Leng Beng in London, and exclaimed over the phone: "Chairman, all hell broke loose! This whole thing is going to break up. Moshe is going to walk out!" With just three months to deadline, Kwek knew that it was too late to find a new architect and start anew. He called Adelson in Las Vegas.

Adelson: "Why are you calling me in bed?"

Kwek: "I think you know what I want to talk to you about."

Adelson: "Are you talking about the ship? It's so expensive and ridiculous! The architecture is not flexible at all."

Kwek: "I'm telling you, you're doing yourself a favour by listening to me. That's why I'm your adviser. If you pull this plan now, you will never get the project. How much is the SkyPark? US$100 million? How much is the total development? This is a fraction of the total building cost. What are you talking about?"

Adelson: "Okay, okay. If you say so. Okay."

Safdie compromised by submitting two versions to Singapore's Urban Redevelopment Authority (URA), one with and one without the SkyPark. He had attached the SkyPark to the towers with removable screws in the model. During the presentation to URA, he never unscrewed Adelson's hated ship. The American gaming mogul was despondent. He felt that he had made a mistake listening to Kwek and Safdie. "I've lost this one. Safdie really let me down," he told a friend. In May 2006, he was proven wrong. Sands won the bid for the integrated resort with the SkyPark design. Today, MBS has transformed into Singapore's architectural and tourism icon, dominating a glittering skyline that charmed the world on Hollywood hits like *Crazy Rich Asians* and the Formula One Singapore Grand Prix.

But as Kwek dropped out of the partnership with Sands and gave up his stake in MBS, so did public knowledge or memory of his involvement. Few knew of his quiet influence which made MBS possible. "I often say I'm indebted to him for the SkyPark," said Safdie in an interview for this book. "Sheldon was a very stubborn man. Once he took a position, it was very hard to move him from it. But he had a great deal of respect for Kwek, and he also knew that Kwek understood Singapore better than him. In his quiet way, Kwek is a powerful, powerful person."

Such is the influence and enigma of a man who sits at the top of one of Asia's richest families, overseeing a conglomerate which deals in everything ranging from building materials to diesel engines, from finance to properties and hotels. But even as his family business Hong Leong enjoys a household name status in Singapore and Malaysia, and his flagship CDL company is held up as a blue-chip bellweather stock on the Singapore stock exchange, Kwek is a man seldom heard in public and even less often seen. A favourite story among business circles was how he was shooed away by the security guard at his own Orchard Hotel in Singapore after turning up one day in a new car. His staff recognised his wheels, not his face.

While he may build or own hotel icons around the world, from The Plaza in New York to The Biltmore Mayfair in London, from the Grand Hyatt in Taipei to the Hilton in Seoul, he slips through his daily life in Singapore largely undisturbed and unmolested in public. Hardly anyone ever approaches him for a photograph or an autograph. In his younger days, it was common to see the tycoon brisk-walking alone down Robinson Road or Cecil Street in the Singapore financial district as he skipped between meetings in buildings he owned. He has never had a bodyguard and flies commercial. "Singapore Airlines is safer than private jets," he explained.

When he spoke in public, it was almost always because of a company results' briefing. On the rare occasions of a media interview, they were called for because of a major business project, such as the launch of his M Social chain of hotels. As former top Singapore civil servant Philip Yeo, who is a director in CDL, said: "Leng Beng is a very serious and quiet guy. He doesn't talk much." Management guru W. Chan Kim, who came up with the Blue Ocean strategy concept and has known Kwek for decades, agreed. "When he talks, he gets to the point and he speaks his mind. He doesn't talk nonsense — no BS, b***s***, you know? He's not the BS type of person," said the INSEAD professor. No surprise then that one of Kwek's favourite mantras is "Work Hard, Talk Less, Do More."

He has certainly done quite a lot. In his hometown, Hong Leong Finance is the largest finance company. At its peak in 2013, nearly one in every five private homes sold in Singapore was built by his property firms, headlined mostly by CDL. His office building Republic Plaza was once the joint tallest in Singapore, and his crown jewel condominium The Sail was at one point the world's tallest residential property. Both remain downtown landmarks. Some of the best hotels in the country are his, including the St. Regis, JW Marriott, W in Sentosa, and the new Singapore EDITION Hotel.

But the signature achievement of Kwek has been to expand his family business far beyond the tiny confines of Singapore. When he took over from his father in 1990 after nearly three decades of tutelage, Hong Leong and its subsidiary companies were largely focused on Singapore with scattered business interests in a few Asian territories, such as Malaysia, the Philippines, Hong Kong, Taiwan and mainland China. Kwek turned it into a bona fide global enterprise with businesses in five continents, including at one point listing his proud hotel empire on the London Stock Exchange — the first Singapore company to do so. He tussled with Donald Trump in New York, was feted by Boris Johnson in London, and did business with Prince Alwaleed bin Talal in the Middle East. As Safdie said, Kwek is a very powerful man. When *Fortune* magazine asked in 1995: "Just who the heck is Kwek?", after the Singaporean had bought the Plaza from Trump, it was both in bemusement and awe.

The question is still relevant today. Just who the heck is Kwek? The success stories of his career are easily tracked and reflected. But the person behind the legend, referred to as "LB" by those near him, remains a quiet mystery to most. This authorised biography attempts to fill the gap, reaching beyond the headlines into the details of his businesses, his beliefs, his habits, his solutions to overcome the biggest challenges, and of course, the secrets of his success.

It was a challenge. Kwek does not lend himself easily to a largely retrospective project. He admitted that he is not a fan of hindsight. Good or bad, one of his self-professed signature strengths is to look, and critically, move forward. "Some people will be 'Your company lost so much at Sincere, how to be cool?' This and that," he said, referring to his company writing off an eye-watering S$1.8 billion in 2021 from its investment in the Chinese firm. "But I'll finish, go on to the next chapter. I don't waste time, because if you're worried, if you're still crying, you can never go on to the next chapter quickly. That's not my policy. My policy is: you can make more money if you move on properly." It applies to his successes too. When asked how he managed to buy the Copthorne and Regal chains of hotels in Europe and United States in the 1990s, he finished telling the stories of these deals worth hundreds of millions of dollars in a few minutes. Job done, let's move on. He seems to detest post-action analysis. Rear view mirrors are a waste of time in his world.

Such a clinical attitude is fuelled partly by impatience. Almost everyone interviewed for this book had a personal story — often fairly humorous — of how he is in a perpetual state of restlessness. "If you travel with him, you must wear running shoes because he used to walk so fast," said long-time CDL group general manager

Chia Ngiang Hong. "When we got off the plane, he walked so fast. He also ate very fast, he didn't want to waste time. Once, when he reached the famous Four Seasons roast duck restaurant in London and saw a long queue, he just walked off. He doesn't want to wait even if food is very good!"

At work, he used to prefer taking stairs over lifts in City House, the former headquarters of his company. "He would scold the lift for being slow!" said his head of corporate affairs Gerry De Silva with a guffaw. Kwek often expects near instant results, delivery or products. His favourite phrase is "quick, quick, quick." Once, he gave De Silva instructions to draft a press release in his office on the 61st floor of Republic Plaza. By the time De Silva took the lift to his own office on the 36th floor in the same building, and sat down at his desk, the phone rang. It was Kwek on the other line, and he asked: "Are you done?" When De Silva replied that he had just reached his work station, Kwek grumbled: "You are always so slow!"

To be fair, he gives as good as he takes. He makes quick decisions and does not dither. He also sets a good example of being fastidiously punctual. It is well known in Hong Leong and CDL that the chairman is not only on time, but he is also almost always early. For the six interviews we conducted with him for this book, he was at least 20 minutes early for every appointment. This applies to everything he attends, from board meetings to social lunches, whether in person or virtual. But the bad news for the others is that once he arrives, he expects the proceedings to begin.

During the COVID-19 pandemic, Kwek had to get used to virtual meetings. He was often a good 10–15 minutes early, and bristled when others logged on closer to the scheduled time, as is the norm, said his nephew Kwek Eik Sheng and group chief operating officer of CDL. "He scolded the guy who signed in last — even though he was five minutes early. The poor chap got it from him," he shared with a rueful smile. Veteran hotelier Daniel Desbaillets said: "For me, he's a natural. What you see is what you get."

What everyone sees is that Kwek is all work, almost no play. While he used to play tennis daily and has a well-known fondness for fast cars, the man is a workaholic. On his days off in Singapore, he visits his hotels to make sure they are in top shape. When he is on vacation, he also tries to visit his hotels, or check out his competition. "My hobby is to visit hotels," he said. There is no sight-seeing when he goes on business trips, said former CDL director Foo See Juan. "I went with him to Sydney to check out some hotels in Blue Mountains to acquire in the late 1980s. I can tell you I didn't get to see the Blue Mountains," he shared. "It was non-stop meetings — with bankers, with agents. He was very business-like." Philip Yeo shared that there has never been a lunch after CDL board meetings. "Other companies will have lunches, karaoke and even brandy. Leng Beng is not that type. No free meal!" he said.

Every opportunity, however outlandish it might be, could be a business opening. Former Singapore Foreign Affairs Minister George

Yeo recalled a rare phone call from Kwek in 2019. The businessman had a piece of land in a good location outside Tokyo. When he heard that Japan's Emperor Akihito had abdicated from his throne and was looking for a new home upon leaving the Imperial Palace, he wanted to sell it to the Emperor. "He said he didn't know anybody and whether I could help," recalled Yeo. "That was probably the only time he asked me for a specific favour. It was an extraordinary idea. I was a bit startled because you don't often offer land to a retired Japanese emperor!" The Japanese sovereign eventually declined the offer. "A common trait among business giants is that you can almost sense that their minds never stop worrying, calculating, assessing," said Yeo. Kwek is *Strictly Business*.

He has no concept of work-life balance. His life is work and there are no boundaries between family and work. His wife Cecilia said that he only talks shop at home. "Every lunch and dinner at home is about his projects. He will ask me about his hotel renovations, his condominium launching, the show flats. He appreciates his properties more than his meals!" she said. Both his sons Sherman and Kingston shared that they did not spend much time with him growing up.

His younger relatives who worked with him in Hong Leong and CDL said that they relate to him mostly as a boss and rarely as an uncle. "His work is all consuming, and therefore, it is very hard to distinguish between him as an uncle and as chairman," said his niece Patricia Yeo, who is group finance director of Hong Leong Investment

Holdings, the holding company of Hong Leong Group. Nephew Kwek Eik Sheng said a family meal with his uncle is virtually a work function. "We'll be talking about work most of the time. I suppose that's what he has most in common with us, right?" he observed. It is thus accurate when *The Business Times* in Singapore called him "one of the hardest-working head honchos around" in 2012.

To tell the story of this maverick businessman, my team at The Nutgraf and I conducted six interviews with Kwek in presidential suites at the Grand Copthorne Waterfront and the St. Regis Singapore and his office in Republic Plaza. While he may be reticent at times, he is also a straight shooter who does not sugarcoat his words, and at times, with a wry sense of humour. During our last interview, he received a scam call on his mobile, and he shouted into the phone: "Hello? This is a police station. Don't disturb me! No disturbing. This is a police station!"

However, the octogenarian had a tendency to jump between topics, and was often reluctant, or unable, to go in-depth into some business deals. Many decisions were made based on his instincts honed from decades of overcoming financial crisis after financial crisis, building an enterprise from an age of abacus to a time of artificial intelligence. To fill in the gaps, I spoke to nearly 30 of his business associates, colleagues and family members. There were hardly any friends on the list because Kwek admitted in our first interview that he has few buddies, if any. One of them, Sir David Michels who used to run the Hilton group of hotels, said: "This is not an easy man to be friendly with. But then some people say I'm not easy either. Understand one thing, he always grumbles. He wakes up, he grumbles: this isn't good enough, that isn't good enough, you don't know how to run a hotel, you don't make enough money for me, it's Thursday. I tell him this and he laughs but it's Leng Beng way of operating."

Unless otherwise stated, all quotes in this book are from these interviews. These are supplemented by my research, including from books, newspapers articles, and company annual reports. This book is divided into 20 chapters across six parts, running on a thematic chronological track. In the first two parts, I have devoted significant space to explore the complex relationship between Kwek and his father, the founder of the Hong Leong group of companies. It lays the foundation for a closer examination and understanding of how Kwek evolved into the businessman he is today.

Part 3 starts from 1990, when he succeeded his father as the leader of the family business and began building his global hotel empire. In Part 4, the reader will see Kwek racing to the peak both at home and abroad, establishing firmly his reputation as an entrepreneur with one of the best feel of the markets in Singapore. This is followed by Part 5 that looks into three major mega projects which he was a part of and all by the waterfront of Singapore. In the last part, the story goes to China and South Korea before addressing the thorny issue of succession. In a few chapters, I broke with regular prose to present the story in listicles and even a Frank Sinatra-

inspired duet of sorts. This is to give readers clearer takeaways from Kwek's life story, which I hope can be applicable to their own careers, enterprises and lives.

Taken together, this biography tells the untold story of one of Singapore's most accomplished businessmen, someone who, to use his words, "planted Singapore's flag" all over the world with his headline acquisitions. Kwek may regard talking as a zero-sum game against doing, but few would quarrel with his style given his achievements over seven decades since the 1960s. *Strictly Business* offers a rare private sector addition to a Singapore Story hitherto dominated by politics and government. Or at the very least, I hope it will help answer the question: "Just who the heck is Kwek?"

Peh Shing Huei

Part 1

The Young Kwek

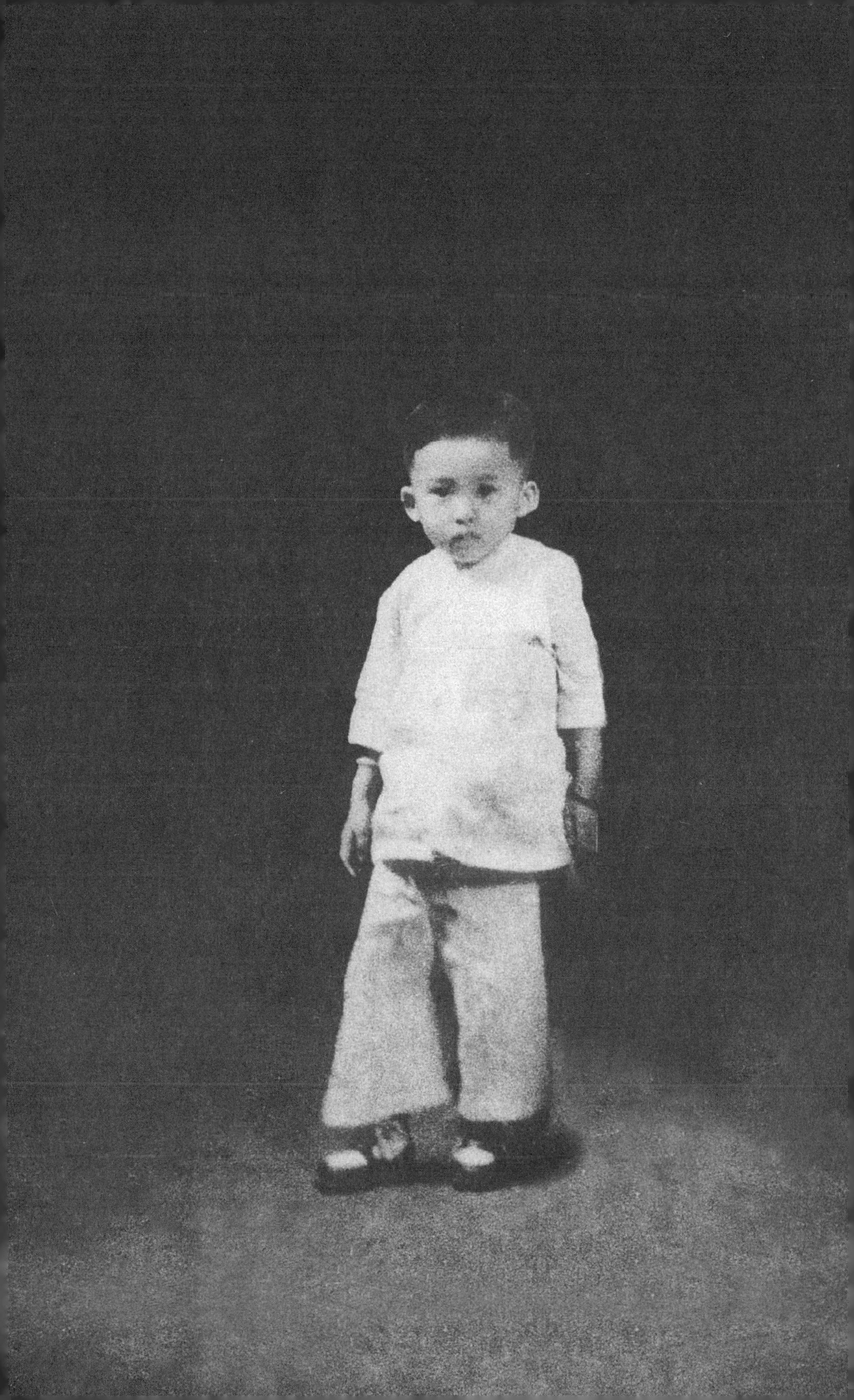

”

Only with hindsight am I now able to appreciate how much I learned from the experience of (my father's) tutelage.

— Kwek Leng Beng

CHAPTER 1

First Pot of Gold

"Having travelled thousands of miles across the seas, the last thing I wanted to do was to go home and admit that I had failed."

— Kwek Hong Png in his autobiography.

When Kwek Hong Png finally sank $7,000 of his life savings into setting up his own company trading in building materials, the boss he was working for was furious. It did not matter that the boss was also his brother-in-law. By setting up a rival firm in the same business, Kwek had crossed a line. The boss was determined to destroy the young upstart. He swore: "I will kill you in the business and make sure you go bankrupt." Kwek was unbowed. After 13 years of service in his brother-in-law's company, the 29-year-old was determined to strike out on his own. "I don't want to disturb you," he replied. "But if you want to fight with me, I'm not scared and I will take you on."

Amid such dark clouds, Hong Leong Company was born in 1941. The name was chosen carefully by the new entrepreneur. He wanted a Chinese name with deep meaning and significance, beyond its connotations of "bountiful harvests." "The name suggests that the company is no average company but a company with high growth potential and an abundance of opportunities to grow from strength to strength," he wrote in his thin pamphlet-like autobiography in Chinese, published in 1987.

Some six months later, in December 1941, the Japanese dropped their first bombs in Singapore. It opened the first chapter to a full-scale invasion in early 1942. The air raid by 17 planes of the Imperial Japanese Navy Air Force left 61 dead and 133 people injured. Kwek could not have chosen a worse time to start Hong Leong. Into this volatile mix of bloodshed, war, and intimidation, Kwek became a father for the second time. His wife, a distant relative whom he had married and brought to Singapore from his hometown in China, gave birth to a son in early 1941. Almost by the fiat of destiny, Kwek Leng Beng arrived in this world irrevocably tied to the fortunes of his father, Hong Leong and the turbulent geopolitics of the 20th century.

No one has shaped Kwek Leng Beng more than his father. He made no bones of his admiration, even adulation, of his old man, despite a challenging relationship which often drove the young Kwek to desperation. During the first discussion on this book project, Kwek Leng Beng said his preference was for a biography on his father, rather than himself. "He was a great man," he said.

Few would argue with his proclamation. When Kwek Hong Png died in 1994, former Singapore Deputy Prime Minister Goh Keng

Swee, the architect of the country's economic success, paid him this tribute: "Quite frankly, only a number of people can achieve the success which Mr Kwek has done, one of several thousand." Fellow Old Guard Cabinet Minister Ong Pang Boon, who was later a director of Hong Leong, echoed the compliments in his foreword to Kwek's memoirs: "The story of Mr Kwek Hong Png, regarded by many as the typical self-made Singaporean entrepreneur, whose rise to prominence in the business world makes fascinating reading. It is the story of a man who overcomes his difficult environment by sheer grit and determination." The story of Kwek Leng Beng has to start with the dramatic rags to riches success of his father.

In 1928, Kwek Hong Png left his impoverished village in Tongan county in southern Fujian province in China for Singapore. He was only 16, with minimal education. His parents were farmers, barely surviving in the harsh post-imperial chaos of China. They bought an eight-dollar ticket for him on a cargo vessel, gave him a quilt and a mat, and sent him off to the British colony in search of a better life, any life. The teenager had only the Singapore address of a brother-in-law as compass. He was almost penniless. The 10-day voyage left such an indelible mark on him that years later in his old age, he could still recall the name of the filthy ship — *Daima Apka*.

When he met his brother-in-law, the man had no idea who the new arrival was. "I haven't seen you before," he said, according to recollections by Kwek in *Leaders of Singapore*. "What are you doing here in Singapore at such a young age?" Kwek Hong Png replied:

"My father is having a hard time in China, and he said maybe I should come to Singapore and become an apprentice, and to study at night." He began as a store hand in his brother-in-law's hardware business, before rising to be a tally clerk, and then a salesman buying and selling goods in Indonesia, Malaysia and Thailand. At night, he studied with a tutor to improve his reading and writing.

By the mid-1930s, the young man had proven himself so adept at his work that he was put in charge of running the business as its general manager. When commodity prices shot up after the Japanese invaded China in 1937, he made a tidy profit for the company and was rewarded with special bonuses. "I was very satisfied with what I had at that time," he said in a 1982 interview with the National Archives of Singapore's Oral History.

But there was a gnawing itch to fulfill a dream shared by many overseas Chinese. "One day when the opportunity comes, and we have the capital, we can become our own boss. At that time, that was my dream," he said in the same interview. He put it more eloquently in his autobiography: "Although I had done well in my job, I felt I could perform better if I were on my own. As the Chinese saying goes, '*It may be a beautiful garden but it isn't home*,' and I dreamt of setting up a garden that I could call my own. I had already worked out the name for my own company. I decided I would call it Hong Leong."

Despite the curses of his brother-in-law, Kwek Hong Png forged ahead with his new company in a shophouse along Beach Road, by the southern waterfront of Singapore. It is a location which his son, Leng Beng, would return to nearly 70 years later with one of his most iconic projects, The South Beach, which is an integrated development of hotel, residences, offices, shops and restaurants. Kwek Hong Png's senior beachfront enterprise was a far humbler and less glamorous business. He ran a general trading firm dealing in paint, ropes, ship and rubber estate supplies, and dabbled a little in foodstuff like rice.

While Kwek Hong Png was forced to stop his new business for months after Japanese troops marched into Singapore in February 1942, he quickly realised that he could not allow fear to consume him. Doing nothing would mean starvation for his young family. As he gradually resumed Hong Leong tepidly, he realised there was an acute shortage of rice in Singapore. Through his contacts built up in trading over the years, he learnt that there was ample supply in Thailand. Instead, what the kingdom lacked was shipping materials, such as thick ropes used to anchor ships. He bought the ropes in Singapore, shipped them to Bangkok on motor *tongkangs*, and exchanged them for rice to be sold back home.

The success gave him confidence that Hong Leong need not close shop during the war. Before the Dutch surrendered Indonesia to the Japanese, he bought paint, iron and steel from Jambi and sold them in Singapore. The buyers? Japanese troops. He was issued a cheque by the Japanese military, which he deposited into the Yokohama Specie Bank. When a cashier, who was a local Chinese and a good friend of his, asked him which currency he preferred to be paid — British or Japanese military notes — he always chose the former. "During the three and a half years, I managed to make a handsome amount of British money," he said in *Leaders*. "I was thinking that the Japanese wouldn't stay here for long. The maximum would be two to three years. So I kept all the British currency. The military notes were for the army. It wasn't the actual currency of Japan. This didn't take much thinking. It was very clear to me. When they surrendered, I think I had more than 10 million military notes. It all became trash. I put them in a bag and threw them away."

He was a savvy investor too. Despite the war, he quickly invested his earnings in properties, houses and plantations. In 1943, in the midst of the Japanese Occupation, he shelled out a princely sum of $43,000 in British colonial currency to buy a 10-year-old bungalow on 25,000 square feet of land at Buckley Road, situated on the outskirts of downtown Singapore. "I didn't have much before the war, just a few thousand dollars," he said. "During the Japanese time, I made quite a huge amount of money. After the Japanese left, I was earning a lot of money. That laid the foundation. That was my beginning."

Kwek Hong Png was living proof of the famous dictum by ancient Chinese thinker Sun Tzu: "In the midst of chaos, there is also opportunity." It is a philosophy which Kwek Leng Beng learnt from his father, and would embrace and execute masterfully as he circumnavigated decades of financial crises, wars, disruptions and even a mysterious epidemic and pandemic. In a speech in 2003, Kwek Leng Beng said: "War or peace, good times or bad times, if you look hard enough there are always opportunities to be had. To put it simply, there is never a good or bad time to start a business." But the war was not without personal costs and tragedy. His wife, and the mother of Kwek Leng Beng, died from shock after a bombing raid. Kwek Hong Png would throw himself into work, leaving the care of his son and daughter Geok Luan to his mother, whom he had brought over from China before the war.

As Hong Leong grew, he realised he needed extra manpower. He turned to his three brothers, whom he had also fetched from China earlier. They were Hong Khai, Hong Lye and Hong Leong. Contrary to a popular misconception, the company Hong Leong was not named after Kwek Hong Png's youngest brother. The two Hong Leongs are written differently in Chinese and have different meanings. In 1996, Kwek Hong Lye was the last of the brothers to pass away. He is the father of Quek Leng Chan, the head of the Hong Leong group in Malaysia, a conglomerate with business interests across Asia.

Kwek Hong Png's sharing of the business with his brothers was fairly unorthodox. Instead of holding on to the majority share, he gave a 65 per cent stake to his three brothers, electing to retain only 35 per cent for himself. "This may seem a very generous act, but to me, it is in accordance with Chinese ethics which likens brothers with fingers on the hand; every finger is a part of one's body and is inseparable," he wrote. "In later years, my faith in my brothers was confirmed over and over again. They underwent many hardships with me and they displayed great stoicism."

Armed with its first pot of gold during the occupation, Hong Leong expanded quickly after the war. As sea-lanes reopened and Singapore embarked on the reconstruction of its ravaged city, Kwek Hong Png swiftly moved into shiphandling and widened its product range in building and construction materials. Critically, the company invested in rubber in 1946. Even by his high standards at this point in his career, this was an astounding venture. "The investments paid off spectacularly," he wrote. When the Korean War broke out four years later in 1950, rubber prices went from 35 cents a pound to $2 a pound. Kwek Hong Png was now a bona fide tycoon, ready to turn Hong Leong into an empire.

CHAPTER 2

Papa Don't Preach

"Leng Beng was a quiet boy who didn't talk much."

— Kwek Geok Luan on her younger brother.

One day in 1968, Kwek Leng Beng had enough. Nothing the 27-year-old man did was good enough for his boss and father. He was too slow, he lacked business nous and he was too conservative. Heck, even the way he crossed cheques irritated his old man. "It was very stressful for me as a young man," he shared. "The pressure from him was too much." He decided to run away. On a whim, and without much thought, he escaped to Penang in Malaysia in a rare act of rebellion. He did not know how long he wanted to stay away or what he was going to do next. All he wanted was a reprieve from the incessant shelling, or in his own words — "*pom, pom, pom, pom, pom.*"

Kwek Hong Png would harangue his eldest son for "being too academic" and having all the wrong attributes for the business world — "naïve, *kiasu*, *kiasi*," the latter two being Hokkien words which mean "afraid to lose" and "afraid of death" respectively. In his Oral

History interview with the National Archives of Singapore, he lamented that his son was "very careful" twice. "My father was so harsh," said Kwek Leng Beng. "I was a junior fellow. He hammered me by saying that 'I don't want you to do this, I want you to do that!' I replied: 'But I haven't learnt how to do it yet.' He would fire back: 'That's always your excuse. You are always saying you haven't learnt enough'. I couldn't win."

Five years after he first joined family business Hong Leong, he would come to realise his legal training at the University of London and certification as a chartered secretary — or company administrator — had left him at odds with his father. The young and quiet Western-trained law graduate wanted his role to be a backend position. "I thought I'd be able to contribute to my old man's business as an administrator because while Chinese companies like his were very good at doing business, they could have used better organisation and more efficient systems," he said in an interview with *The Straits Times* in 2004. "But my father said: 'I don't care how good your administration and systems are, if you don't have sales, you don't have income and if you don't have income, you're dead'."

Kwek admitted decades later he dreaded working for his father. All his ideas for the family business Hong Leong were rejected in the early years. "You couldn't discuss or offer any ideas. He was the king. Whatever I wanted to offer, any strategy, any idea, was below his standards," he said. "He would say: 'You shut up! Don't offer me anything below my standards'." His father said as much in his Oral

History interview. When asked if his sons would go against his decisions in business, Kwek Hong Png replied: "No, no, they dared not. I contributed my ideas to them mostly. I would suggest that they do it this way. But actually, my thinking is never wrong."

The patriarch, like many men of his time, ran the family and the business with near absolute control, with more than a little fear thrown in the mix, observed Kwek Leng Beng's wife Cecilia. "My father-in-law was very tough on my husband," she recalled. "Every time, every day, every hour, he would push him. And he wouldn't give him the reason why he's doing that. In other words, he's very dictatorial. So the poor son had no idea what it was all about. Maybe sometimes as a young man, he would take it easy. Then he would get scolded."

Kwek Leng Beng often returned home in the evenings drained from a day of pummeling by his father. "Often, I could see he had a really tough day," said Cecilia Kwek, who was born in Malaysia and trained in law in London like her husband. "I was all behind him and I told him your father is training you. What you don't understand, try to ask him when he's in a good mood. If he's in a bad mood, just walk away and don't answer back. That is Chinese tradition." Communication between father and son was limited, patience in even shorter supply. In the eyes of the Kwek patriarch, children were truly meant to be seen and not heard — even if they were already in their late 20s. "Don't ask too much. Just observe," said Kwek Leng Beng. "He had no patience. He would be annoyed.

You should learn on your own. He was a man who said very little."

The control extended beyond work. Date nights with Cecilia had to end by 9pm. "The old man wanted him to be in bed by 9pm. He dictated bedtime," she shared. "He wanted him well rested for tomorrow's business. When my husband's face was rather pale — 'oh you didn't sleep well.' When his face was ruddy — 'oh you drank?' The old man was quite extreme. From the beginning, he wanted to train my husband to be the successor and he was really old school."

Kwek Leng Beng often talked about running away from home, said his wife. But the escape to Penang was short-lived. A good friend of his father was a resident in the city, and he slowly persuaded the young man to return home. "He said: 'He is your father and he meant well. Why do you run away? Running away is not a challenge. Accept it as a challenge. Any problem, call me'," recalled Kwek. When he got home, his father kept quiet and did not put him through a lecture. The hatchet was buried. Kwek began to understand the sacrifices his father made and embraced the challenges. "I accepted he was harsh. But at the end of a harsh day, you could find a silver lining," he said. "I was no longer frightened."

The turning point would set him on a two-decades-long learning journey under his father, until he took over Hong Leong in 1990. Along the way, he quietly watched, absorbed and applied, and by the time the long shadows of his father had receded in the 21st century, Kwek had morphed into one of the best and most ardent disciples of his father. In almost every major speech, publication and interview, he never failed to give credit to the man who started the company.

In a speech in 2010, he hailed his father as the "Guru of Real Estate" in Singapore. "Only with hindsight am I now able to appreciate how much I learned from the experience of his tutelage. I benefitted by observing him at work, watching how he took important decisions — sometimes intuitively, sometimes drawing on his insight and witnessing how he was able to draw on his understanding and experience of the real estate business," he added. "He instilled strong values in me, in my brother and our cousins, by teaching us financial prudence and instilling in us a deep and critical knowledge of the real estate business. He led by example, showing us how to be fair and consistent in our dealings and how to stay at all times very focused."

To those who have watched Kwek since young, the clues were fairly obvious that he would evolve into his father's Mini-Me. He was obedient, disciplined, and, yes, very focused. "He would always sit down in a corner and read his books before he went to school," recalled his older sister Kwek Geok Luan. "He was a very hardworking and good boy who didn't give any trouble." Although his mother passed away when he was young, and his father was mostly busy with work, his childhood was a blissful one. He was brought up by his grandmother in a shophouse along the Singapore River. "I was very loved by my grandmother," he said. "Even when it was a very hot day, she would put a lot of clothing on me and so I became very hot and sweaty. It was her way of showing love for you."

At five, after the war, he moved into his father's new bungalow in Buckley Road, a compound shared with his uncles, aunties and several cousins. "We have very happy memories of those days," said Kwek Geok Luan. "We were all very innocent and it was plenty of fun having the whole family living together. My brother was a quiet boy who didn't talk much. He would play with our cousins in the evening, cycling and playing ball." Soon thereafter, his father remarried and three younger siblings joined the family — brother Leng Joo, and two sisters.

Kwek Leng Beng studied in Beatty Primary School and Bartley Secondary School before heading to London to read law. There, he began to take on a new role as leader of his extended family, exhibiting for the first time the traits of his father which had hitherto been latent. As his cousins joined him in the British capital for studies, he became what he described as the "captain" of a team of young Kweks. And like his old man, he was strict, frugal and disciplined, said family friend and London flatmate Yeoh Cheng Kung, who later became a lifelong employee. "He was so frugal that I had no idea how rich his family was when we first met," he recalled. "We rented a shabby apartment together. I remember he hardly spent money!"

He frowned on his cousins dining out, insisting it was cheaper to cook at home. On occasions, the younger ones would sneak out, seeking the greasy gourmet delights of London's Chinatown. When they returned, Kwek would sniff their winter coats for the faintest smell of food. "They couldn't bluff me," he said. "I would bark: 'Where did you go?' I was strict."

On weekends, his idea of a day out was to corral his cousins to a library to study. "He was a no-nonsense guy who didn't like to waste time," said Yeoh. "He was very disciplined even at that point in his life, and except for the occasional tea dances, I cannot remember him doing anything fun. The rest of us would play mahjong, poker and drink. He didn't do anything except study. He was a serious guy." When Kwek finally left London for Singapore, his cousins sent him off at the airport with playful cheers of "*Merdeka*! *Merdeka*!" — independence, from the young boss.

Kwek returned home to report to the original commander. As he joined the family business in 1963 as an entry-level management executive, it coincided with Singapore's merger with Malaya to form Malaysia. The young returnee was soon despatched by his father to Malaysia to start Hong Leong's branch in Kuala Lumpur. Despite having a law degree, Kwek never considered practising. "Why do you want to be a lawyer? How much can a lawyer earn? Why would I want to be a lawyer when my mind was independent and I could seize opportunities?" he asked rhetorically. "I learnt from my father, however harsh he was." He had the option of not joining Hong Leong. "But I was thinking to myself: 'Why would I want to kick myself out?' I don't think I could learn as much outside on my own," he said.

By then, Hong Leong had transformed into a formidable business in building materials. In 1956, it set up joint ventures with Japanese industrialists, in particular Mitsui and Onoda Cement, to import cement for the growing industrialisation of Singapore and Malaya. Mitsui is one of the largest conglomerates in the world, and its early tie-up with the Kweks would kick off a thriving partnership that lasts till today. In 1962, Hong Leong would set up the first cement plant in Singapore, producing 180,000 tons a year — enough not only for all of the city's needs, but also with some excess for export. The $6-million factory, said Kwek, "created a sensation" and its announcement was front-page news in Singapore newspapers.

In 1965, when Singapore split from Malaysia and gained its independence, Kwek was recalled by his father to return to his hometown. His cousin, Quek Leng Chan, who also studied law in London, was sent in his place to Kuala Lumpur to run the business there. Eight years later, Hong Leong Malaysia was hived off into an independent entity under the leadership of Quek and his branch of the family. Their surnames are spelt differently because of different romanisations of their same Chinese family name.

Despite his misgivings working with his father, Kwek's return from Malaysia would herald his embrace of and ascension in the world of business — notwithstanding the 1968 escape to Penang. He would be shaped increasingly into the mould of the founder of Hong Leong, harbingering an early insight into the upcoming smooth succession from first-generation leaders to the second. He said in an interview in 2018: "There were several people who had significant influence on me, but the person who had the biggest impact was my late father. He was a true entrepreneur with big vision and lots of gravitas, yet very disciplined and pragmatic. He taught me many things that shaped my business philosophy and how I should lead my life."

His work ethic began to mirror his father's fairly quickly. Once, in the 1960s, his then girlfriend Cecilia brought him legal documents to sign. She was working in a law firm which serviced Hong Leong. When Kwek discovered a calculation error in the document, he threw the file at her — romantic interest was clearly not above professional duties. "I quickly ran out of the office. I didn't know what to do!" said Cecilia Kwek, laughing at the memory. "I didn't question him after that and he didn't bring it up too." Privately, the young man also became increasingly similar to his father. While he was Western-educated, his wife described his dating style as traditional and old school. "No roses and chocolates from him," she laughed. "He was not that type. We would go out for dinners and even then he would always be talking about work. He was in awe of the old man."

When it was pointed out to Kwek Leng Beng in an interview for this book that his business thinking, strategic approaches and life decisions have been remarkably similar to his dad, he afforded himself a rare wry smile, before replying: "Birds of the same kind flock together. Inevitably, after observing for so long, it goes into my head."

Part 2

On the Job Training

”

I was so hungry for business that I personally drove my staff to the streets in South Bridge Road and Thomson Road and asked them to knock on doors and not to come back until every single business establishment had been approached.

— Kwek Leng Beng

CHAPTER 3

Hit the Ground

"He doesn't like to see you in the office. You are supposed to be out on the field, getting business!"

— former Hong Leong Finance senior vice-president James Sim.

Soon after joining Hong Leong Finance as a branch manager in 1971, James Sim was offered a ride by his young boss Kwek Leng Beng. It was a rare chance to enjoy the breeze in a gleaming grey Jaguar convertible, at a time when such luxury automobiles remained as infrequently sighted in Singapore as the big cat whom the brand was named after. Sim hopped in at their corporate headquarters in Robinson Road, the central business district of Singapore, and Kwek drove east.

When they reached Lavender Street, an area packed with shops selling hardware and building materials — not far from Beach Road where Kwek's father had first set up Hong Leong — the driver told the passenger he had reached his destination. "Go to the shops and get some business," Kwek told Sim. "I will be back in an hour and you can tell me what you have done." Surprised, but undeterred, Sim gamely trooped to the shops and introduced himself as a Hong Leong

Finance employee. Before he could go on, the hardware shopkeepers turned hostile. "I was literally thrown out!" said Sim. "They saw me as a competitor. They thought I was a spy." Hong Leong, after all, had first made its name in the hardware and building materials business. "I was truly quite dismayed," said Sim. "I thought it was a big joke asking me to get business from competitors."

Kwek duly circled back in an hour to find a grumpy employee waiting by the roadside. Sim told him the unceremonious receptions he had received, expecting some sympathy from the boss. Instead, Kwek laughed: "So easily defeated! Try again." Like a bad joke, he drove Sim back to the same place the next day. Grudgingly, Sim approached the same shops. Not surprisingly, the result was the same. "I was thrown out again," he recalled with a wince.

Sim wanted to give up, but Kwek would have none of it. The next day, for the third time, the managing director of Hong Leong Finance drove Sim back to same place, dropped him off, and made him try again. Sim was determined not to be turned down again. He pleaded with the shopkeepers: "Please give me a chance, or I will be out of a job very soon." This time, they agreed to at least hear out his elevator pitch. Sim was prepared. Hong Leong Finance wanted to extend loans to these companies. But these business owners said they did not need credit. Sim offered: "Take $50,000 and if you don't need or want it, you can close the account. No charges." He clinched his first deal. "I learnt that day that I was working for a man who would never say die. I had to learn to be more thick-skinned," said Sim.

In 1966, Hong Leong moved into the finance world and the young Kwek was quickly tasked to run this new subsidiary in the fast-growing group. It was a rude awakening to the world of retail business for the 25-year-old. He learnt the hard way that not only are there no short-cuts to success, but there are also plenty of rough cuts when operating in the fairly cut-throat world of small and medium-sized enterprises (SMEs) in a newly-independent and struggling Singapore. The lessons he picked up when he hit the ground would provide the ballast that would eventually lead him to global success.

In no time, he realised his father was right. No amount of systems and organisations can help a business if there are no sales. Legend has it in Hong Leong Finance that when Kwek first started work, he spent a few days sitting in the company's office before learning that there were no clients walking in. He would say many years later: "I have a philosophy. Business doesn't come automatically. You have to go out to hunt for business."

In the first place, unlike a bank, many Singaporeans had little inkling what a finance company was in those early days of economic development, said Kwek. "They saw us as credit companies or worse, petty moneylenders only to turn to when all their options have run out," he said in an interview with *The Business Times* in 2003. The only way out is to go out. "I was so hungry for business that I personally drove my staff to the streets in South Bridge Road and Thomson Road and asked them to knock on doors and not to come back until every single business establishment had been approached." Sim was one of them. He said: "Customers said we were not a bank, so what did a finance company sell?"

Kwek learnt to be aggressive. While banks have a wider scope of activities, finance companies operate on a tighter and shorter leash. Generally, loans from a finance company are fully collaterised according to regulatory requirements. However, borrowers are also assessed on a criteria that includes credit worthiness and repayment ability subject to the type and purpose of the loans required. Such restrictions naturally limit finance companies' clients to those who have been rejected by the banks. Or in Singapore's case, the smaller of the SMEs. To get their businesses, Hong Leong Finance must reach out and be creative. When the company struggled for business after opening a branch in rural northern Nee Soon, Kwek suggested to Sim to organise film screenings and operas to build relationships with the community. They would follow up with baby shows and ping pong tournaments to gain customers.

Such rough terrain also brought with it some unsavoury types. Kwek was not afraid to give it as hard as he took it, even though he was only in his 20s. Once, a customer had reported the loss of an original certificate and obtained a duplicate. He then tried to use both certificates to obtain a loan, looking for double the amount. When the counter staff at Hong Leong Finance refused, he began to holler: "What kind of lousy company is this? You dare not lend me money. I came here with two certificates, but you only want to pay me for one." Kwek came out to the front desk and confronted the man.

He said: "Boss, don't frighten my new staff. I can report this to the police and you will be in trouble."

The customer replied: "Go ahead, I'm not scared."

"How can you try to do something like that?"

"I have dealt with your uncle many times, so you shut up!"

"No, you shut up. If you don't stop, I will fight with you."

"I will take my business elsewhere."

"Thank you very much, I don't want your business."

In another instance, a client came storming in, upset that Hong Leong Finance had sold his shares without his permission. He had pledged his shares for a loan. The finance company was allowed to dispose of the collateral if it deemed that the shares were falling below a certain value. "He was so angry," recalled Kwek. "He shouted at me 'what goes down could go up'. I told him what goes down could also go down further and that was my assessment. At least I preserved his capital." Kwek called security guards to his side, afraid that the man was about to turn violent. Months later, the customer returned and demanded to see Kwek again. The young boss summoned the security guards again. "I thought he was going to punch me!" Instead, the client thanked Kwek. "If you hadn't sold, the shares would have gone down even further and I would have lost my capital," he said.

Such frontline action of the most in-your-face form of retail business became the best training ground for the young entrepreneur.

Not only was it challenging, but it was also humbling for the son of a tycoon. There were no deals too small and there were no problems too minor. His aggressive and on-the-ground tactics quickly paid off, and in 1969, Hong Leong Finance was listed on the Stock Exchange of Singapore and Malaysia. A decade later, in 1979, it won a brutal six-month bidding war to buy rival Singapore Finance, edging out United Overseas Bank. The acquisition turned Hong Leong Finance into the largest finance company in Singapore with assets totaling about S$350 million. The group had 18 branches, a spread greater than most of the local banks.

Along the way, Kwek picked up five important lessons that he would carry with him for the rest of his career, from property to hospitality.

▶ Lesson 1: Sales is the lifeblood of a business

It was a mantra Kwek learnt in Hong Leong Finance and it was a lesson he passed on to all his staff in the company. As the firm's former president Ian MacDonald said: "Everything is about sales." And the chief salesman was Kwek himself. "He loves to be a salesman and would wait for an appropriate time to ask for your business." Sometimes, it may be completely unplanned.

In 2003, MacDonald was visiting the Porsche service centre at the western end of Singapore for a business meeting. He was there to pitch to car dealer Eurokars Group, whose brands in Singapore include Rolls-Royce, Porsche and Mini, offering car loans to the distributorship's clients. When MacDonald and a young staff walked into the compound, they bumped into Kwek test driving the then new Porsche Cayenne, the first time the famous sports car brand had gone four doors with a sports utility vehicle. In the passenger seat was Karsono Kwee, the boss of Eurokars. When Kwek found out from MacDonald the purpose of his visit, he asked: "Can I sit in the meeting?"

Of course, MacDonald could not refuse. "The young guy I was with was absolutely petrified," he said with a laugh. "He was going to do the presentation and now suddenly the chairman of our company was going to sit in." Thankfully, barely five slides into the PowerPoint presentation, Kwek, as usual, ran out of patience. He stood up, excused himself, and as he was about to step out, turned back to Kwee and thundered: "Karsono, give us the business!"

The deal was sealed and till today, Eurokars remains a client of Hong Leong Finance, said MacDonald, relishing the retelling of this 20-year-old anecdote like it happened yesterday. "We had a leader who was not just directing activities, but where possible, would be intimately involved," he said. "You could tell he enjoyed being the chief salesman."

▶ Lesson 2: Decide, because that's the job of a boss

It might sound obvious to some, but too often, many bosses either do not want to decide or they are too afraid to do so. The weight of responsibility can often be paralysing. Not for Kwek. He learnt early on that his main job as a boss was to decide, and he would not waver. That did not mean he made his calls without proper research and consultation. "He's a cautious man, make no mistake," shared Soon Yee Christie, former group financial controller of Hong Leong Finance who worked in the company for 34 years. "If we could grant 30 per cent, he would cut it to 25 per cent. He always built in a margin," she said. "He's decisive in that he wanted to have the answers yesterday."

When he wanted to hire a senior manager, he moved quickly and did not outsource the decision making. Hong Leong Finance president Ang Tang Chor recalled a 90-minute job interview with Kwek, where he was peppered with plenty of both real and hypothetical questions about the finance sector and SMEs. By the end of the interview, Kwek had made his call. "You're on board," he told Ang.

Once, when Hong Leong Finance was about to lose a major client, MacDonald managed to get a pledge from the customer that it would stay with them if Hong Leong Finance could match a rival financial institution's offer. But such favourable terms could be signed off by only Kwek, and the deadline was on the day itself. "It was a bit of a tall order from the client," said MacDonald. He asked for an appointment from Kwek but was told that the boss was all booked up for the day. After repeating exhortations, the secretary finally relented: "You have five minutes. Come to the boardroom at 4.17pm."

On the dot, Kwek came out of the boardroom, asked MacDonald "the most salient questions," and then made the decision to grant the special terms. He returned to the boardroom in five minutes. The next day, MacDonald read in the morning papers that Kwek's meeting was to ink the deal to buy the land to build The Sail, Singapore's tallest condominium. "He was still totally focused on Hong Leong Finance in that five minutes, gave me time, and made a decision," he said.

▶ Lesson 3: Be hands-on and get your hands dirty

Despite being a tycoon and one of the richest men in Asia, Kwek believed in, and enjoyed, getting involved in his businesses. It was a habit he picked up from managing Hong Leong Finance. Kwek chaired the loans approving authority of Hong Leong Finance and personally signed off on all the major deals, said the group president Ang Tang Chor. "He was very seldom wrong," he said. While the company would suffer losses from individual loans every now and then, Kwek ensured it maintained a profitable portfolio. Said Christie: "He was definitely proven correct more often than not. It's jolly hard work when you have to look at the loans on a case-by-case basis, but there were hardly any lapses on his part."

When he decided to focus a big chunk of Hong Leong Finance's business on motor vehicle loans, he would frequently visit car dealerships like Eurokars to learn more about the car business, said Ang. "He would know which are the models selling well, how

Hong Leong Finance's loans compared with our competitors, which are the most popular loans," he said. "So when he asked us for information about the clients, you better know your stuff. Tell him the wrong things, and you would get it. He was a boss who was extremely hands-on and so he knew his stuff. Don't try to hoodwink him. I had learnt that if I didn't know anything, it was best to be upfront and admit it, then try my best to find out quickly after that."

Kwek was not afraid to dive deep into the minutiae, said nephew Kevin Hangchi, a lawyer who is a director in Hong Leong Finance. "He is a real stickler for detail, insisting that information in his documents must be accurate," he shared. "He had a good memory too. Any doubt, however, would often lead to a massive turnout of documents to get to the facts. Unsurprisingly, my work with him often led to a multitude of draft versions which, on good days would run into the teens, and on not-so-good days would run many times beyond that." This was partly because of Kwek's legal training, he added. "His legal competence and able appreciation for commercial and legal risks is what sets him apart from many other entrepreneurs. I do believe that this has been an important factor that has contributed to his success and reputation."

▶ Lesson 4: Learn about everything; it will come in handy

Kwek built up an insatiable appetite to learn about anything and everything, knowing that they could be useful when assessing loans in Hong Leong Finance. His wealth of experience in the property market eventually gave him and the company a solid foundation to make crucial calls, said Christie. "You got to know that he not only knew residential, but he also understood commercial and industrial properties, including those on 30-year leases by the government," she said. "And the biggest collateral for most of our clients is their properties. His knowledge on this field has served him extremely well." Similarly, his understanding of the stock market and even the motor vehicle business gave him the information he needed to make, yes, decisions.

This applied to the government too. He paid close attention to policies and their changes, and often was willing to concede that the government knew better. "He always accepted that the authorities may know something which we may not yet know," said Christie. At the heart of it was a deep trust of the Singapore government. "He wanted to know what the authorities wanted, especially when the Monetary Authority of Singapore was involved. He believed it was wise to comply."

▶ Lesson 5: Everyone is a possible customer

There is a cliché saying: "When all you have is a hammer, everything looks like a nail." The saying can be adapted somewhat for Kwek. In his case, it is: "When you are a businessman, everyone is a possible customer." He was relentless as the head of Hong Leong Finance. No business was too small for him, said those who worked with him. "One of his favourite tactics was to tell the client that they didn't have to give us all their businesses, just a bit would do," said MacDonald.

Sim recalled an incident in the early 1980s, when German camera maker Rollei had to retrench workers in Singapore. Hong Leong Finance gave a talk to the staff on financing new businesses. One of those who lost his job wanted to set up a computer school business, but no banks would loan him money to buy computers. He had no track record, and computers were new technology then with little resale value.

When Sim brought the case to Kwek, the boss countered that if the client was willing to be a personal guarantor to the loan, Hong Leong Finance was prepared to offer credit. Kwek said to Sim: "Tell the man that if he has confidence in his own business venture, then he should be the guarantor. If not, he should not go into business." The loan was made, and the company Informatics eventually listed on the Singapore Stock Exchange, before running into trouble in the early 2000s.

Kwek also had no aversion to finding customers even among his rivals, as Sim first discovered in Lavender Street. When Kwek put on his Hong Leong Finance hat, he was thinking mainly about the company, and it did not bother him one iota to lend money to those in the building materials business or even fellow property developers later, said MacDonald. "Most of our major clients were developers and they were the rivals of City Developments," he recalled. On the flip side, these developers were also quite happy to borrow from Hong Leong Finance. "It was one of the great puzzles I had in my mind for years," said MacDonald. "I wondered why these developers would come to us because they had to give us all the information which were private and confidential to their businesses."

Eventually, during a Lunar New Year lunch, he plucked up enough courage to ask a developer who was also a client. The reply has stayed with MacDonald for years: "I would always go to Hong Leong Finance precisely because I knew my loan would have to be personally approved by Kwek Leng Beng. If the person who is the best in the business would approve the loan, that means my project is on solid ground." Even his competitors were looking to Kwek for his imprimatur.

These lessons helped Kwek drive Hong Leong Finance from the mid-1960s into the 21st century, turning it into the biggest finance company in Singapore. The firm remained creative with its business by finding a niche not occupied by the banks. It has entrenched itself in the SME sector in Singapore, introducing inventory financing and debt financing, among others. The strategy was paired with the locations of its branches, occupying the public housing heartlands of the country, said Christie. "We moved with the customers."

Former Minister for Trade and Industry (MTI) George Yeo believed that Kwek's early years with Hong Leong Finance shaped his views on SMEs. "He developed a feel for the small and medium enterprises. And I remember him telling me when I was in MTI how we could have done more in helping to finance small and medium enterprises. He did not write them off as lost causes, but he saw in them hope and opportunity. And this was something he learned in his youth." While Kwek is well-known for being a dispassionate businessman, Yeo observed an attachment to Hong Leong Finance. "To me, he has always been practical," he said. "I don't think he's emotional about specific brands. Where I saw him express emotion, it was in Hong Leong Finance, which he built up as a young man. It was probably the first time he crawled out from his father's shadow, and he succeeded."

Even though Kwek's father longed for a banking licence and the authorities' refusal to grant Hong Leong one had irked the patriarch, Kwek had no such desire. "It was always the wish of my father to get one. But I have never dreamt of one. I saw no purpose in it," he said. "As a finance company, I can run it the way I want to run it. I saw no advantage to get a banking licence because I would have to compete with many banks, many big banks. It's better for me to swim in a smaller pond where my fish is the biggest. Do the things you do well and be the leader in the market." This mantra would prove to be true as he pushed his family business into the property market in a big way.

Chapter 4

Only One Cent

"They bought CDL and built it up into the behemoth that it is."

— Far East Organization CEO Philip Ng.

When racial riots broke out in Kuala Lumpur in Malaysia in 1969 and spilled over to neighbouring Singapore, it was the final blow to beleaguered small property developer City Developments Limited. Seven days of clashes between Malay mobs and Chinese triads in Singapore left some 80 injured and four dead. Investors' confidence, already at a low after the 1967 announcement by the British of their military withdrawal east of Suez, sank even lower. City Developments, or CDL as it is popularly known, was frantically trying to channel funds from its moribund Malaysian projects in southern Johor Bahru to Singapore, but its liquidity was extremely tight. It was desperate.

To salvage its business, the publicly listed company on the Stock Exchange of Malaysia and Singapore offered a block of shares for sale. Through a noted stockbroker, word of the offer got to Kwek Leng Beng. "I felt that this was a chance of a lifetime," he said. "With a stroke of a pen, we could build up a formidable land bank." Well, it was not quite a deal that could be settled simply with stationery. There was still the not-so-small matter of an offer price.

Intrigued, Kwek brought the deal to his father and urged the boss to buy. Hong Leong had been making forays into the real estate business and buying CDL would give them a proper foothold. The patriarch took out his abacus, did some quick calculations, and decided that his son was right. It was a good deal. CDL's shares had closed at 41 cents and Kwek senior agreed that it was a worthwhile purchase. Kwek asked for allowance in case the counter should open higher the next day, and his father agreed to a tiny buffer. "I will give you an additional one cent — 42 cents. Buy it tomorrow," Kwek Hong Png ordered.

Alas, the next day, when the market opened, CDL traded at 43 cents, a cent above what his father had instructed as the purchase price. Kwek hesitated. The stockbroker gave him an ultimatum: "Do you want it? If you don't want, somebody else will buy it." Kwek knew he had no time to check back with his father. He had to seize it or lose it. At that moment, he took the plunge that would in many ways change his life forever. "I will take it," he said. In his heart, as he would recall more than half a century later, he knew he had made the right call. Yet, he also felt a familiar ache and dread. "I knew I was going to be scolded," he said.

His prediction was absolutely right, unfortunately. When his father learnt that his son had paid an extra cent more than what he had authorised, he was furious. "Oh, he was unhappy, he scolded me like hell," he said, without a trace of bitterness or irony, even though the Kweks had just pulled off one of the biggest coups in Singapore's corporate history. "I knew that we had gotten a fantastic deal of a lifetime. Let him scold me, never mind!"

The post-Penang young Kwek, who was only 28 years old, was prepared for the shellacking and now had the maturity to deal with it. He admitted he had gone beyond his remit and apologised: "I said 'sorry dad, next time I won't do it *ah*. I made a mistake, *lah*'. The mistake was mine, not his. So he was, in some way, quite happy that I said I learnt my lesson. Without making mistakes, I would never learn my lesson."

And just like that, amid a terrible scolding, one of Singapore's most enduring bellwether stocks would begin its transition into new hands, taking its first step towards being a blue chip and a household name in the country. Although CDL was in a bad shape, it had a lot going for it, positives which drew Kwek to the company: "Most of CDL's land were in very good locations in Singapore — prime areas," he said. "They also had lots of good plans already in place." The problem for CDL was that while it was long on ideas and plans, it was short on funds and even more anaemic in business planning. "I saw a company that was full of potential," said Kwek. "But it was run by professional people and not business people."

The firm was set up in 1963, with a small rented office in Amber Mansions, standing where the present-day Dhoby Ghaut subway station is, along the famous Orchard Road shopping belt in Singapore. It had only eight employees and a board drawn from the British and Chinese communities. CDL's first management team was headed by a British chartered quantity surveyor. To raise capital, it went public just two months after formation. The success quickly led CDL to complete its first housing project called Fresh Breezes in Johor Bahru. The innovative team was even among the first to introduce the "show flat" concept in local real estate marketing.

But for a firm set up nine days before Singapore officially merged with Malaya, and created with an eye on the common Malaysian market, the disintegration of the two territories two years later in 1965 was a major disruption. CDL's two developments in Johor Bahru were badly hit after separation, with the Malaysian property market exceptionally depressed. By June 1966, the Johor Bahru property market had virtually collapsed.

Hong Leong's equity entry was the white knight CDL was craving for. The Kweks put three people on the CDL's board of directors from October 1969, among them Kwek Leng Beng. A rescue package was put forward to solve CDL's cash flow problems, and Kwek got down to untangle the knots which had tied up CDL. For instance, its most promising project in Singapore was Clementi Park on the western part of the island, but the residential development had encountered persistent problems in clearing squatters and tenant farmers. "They drew up a plan, kept on refining the plan, but there were sitting tenants in there," said Kwek. "If you don't get rid of the sitting tenants, you can never develop!"

He made sure the relocation of the tenants was the top priority, pushed for negotiations and compensation, and completed the clearing out quickly. "The CDL folk didn't know how to negotiate with the tenants. So they were held to ransom," he said. "Instead, they kept spending money, beautiful amounts of money, on beautiful designs. But they could not build. That's why I said they were good professional people with good plans, but they were not business people who could solve problems on the ground."

Clementi Park became CDL's most prominent calling card in Singapore for this relatively new housing concept called condominiums. When Kwek felt that there was a lack of local expertise, he hired a leading American architect to plan and develop the latter phases of the project, one which stretched across more than 100 acres of land. CDL soon established a reputation as a reliable developer of high-quality housing. "Hong Leong started in the building materials business, so we were very familiar with quality and costs of construction," he said. "We decided very early on when we moved into real estate that we wanted to establish a reputation in the market. I didn't want to just make money. I wanted our homes to have quality. Some developers just passed the buck to the buyers especially in the 1970s and let them deal with it. That was not how we wanted to build CDL."

In 1972, Hong Leong acquired a majority stake in CDL, the first Western-style corporate takeover by the company. Kwek was tasked to plan and execute the exercise, completing his first corporate acquisition. Observers praised the move. "It is no surprise that the far-sighted Hong Leong Group took control before someone else did," wrote the *New Nation*. The new CDL quickly diversified beyond residential development, adding investment, industrial and commercial properties to its portfolio. *The Straits Times* noticed in a headline that year: "City Dev goes on a land buying spree." A year later, the company had made such a dramatic turnaround that it was able to give out dividends for the first time to its shareholders.

After the oil crisis hit in 1973, Hong Leong took control of the management of the company. Kwek Hong Png became the chairman in 1974 and Kwek Leng Beng was appointed managing director. CDL rode the wave of development in Singapore and transformed into a property powerhouse that garnered more and more attention from the public and the market. In 1980, *The Business Times* reported: "The excitement in the market this week over City Developments comes in the wake of investors' realisation and appreciation of the vast potential of this once-neglected counter…It is on the threshold of embarking on big quality projects which will change fundamentally City's corporate state in the next few years."

In the next decade, CDL would cement its reputation in Singapore as not only a serious major player in real estate, but also an ethical one that believed in quality, sustainability and even buyers' interests. Kwek Leng Beng led the push. In the early 1980s, he joined other property developers in the Real Estate Developers' Association of

Singapore (REDAS) to improve the credibility of industry. At that point, a major problem was the lack of regulations on developers' use of funds collected from buyers. In other words, after receiving payment from buyers on a property, the developer could take the money and use it for other purposes. When the developer then ran into financial difficulties, and could not complete the housing project, buyers would be left without their property.

While such norms favoured developers like CDL, Kwek thought it was unhealthy in the long run and "extremely vulnerable" for buyers. "Like my father, I took a long-term view," he shared. "If buyers are protected, they are likely to buy more. It is good for the public, good for the economy and ultimately good for business." He pushed to set up new rules, restricting the use of the monies collected to the specific property project. The regulations still apply today. "The new rules went a long way to safeguard buyers' money and brought credibility to developers," he said in an interview in 2018, adding that the change remains one of his proudest career achievements.

Gradually, riding on the CDL vehicle, he had found his groove in the world of business. As the company rose in prominence, it began to overshadow Hong Leong as a leading brand in Singapore — a journey which would not have happened if not for the bold move to invest in the firm back in 1969. Looking back, Kwek said it was a critical milestone for him: "It was a feat for a young man like me who was excited about the concept of takeovers both in theory and in practice," he said in the same interview. "That could be the point I found my destiny, besides being the son of my father."

It was a point in his life that could have turned out very differently, if not for the extra cent that he decided to pay. "If you look back, it was a really good buy," he said, with the slightest of a smile.

CHAPTER 5

The King's and I

"King's Hotel is his first love. You never forget your first love."

—former King's Hotel general manager Yeoh Cheng Kung.

When the jet age finally reached Asia in the early 1960s, it was obvious to the young Singapore government that the British colony was unprepared to tap on the good value to be made from global tourism. Jetliners were moving people across borders at a rate unseen in human history, with a record 58 million travellers in 1963, but Singapore had done next to nothing to promote international tourism. Something had to change.

In 1964, the Singapore Tourist Promotion Board (STPB) was set up, with the country's economic czar Goh Keng Swee promising to put some serious government muscles behind the industry. "Everybody knows the great potential of tourism in Singapore by virtue of its international name, and its strategic location on international air and shipping routes," he said in Parliament in 1964. "This potential needs to be exploited through positive measures to promote its growth, and these are best carried out by joint efforts of both private business and government."

Kwek Hong Png and Kwek Leng Beng were watching and listening intently. It was clear that tourism would be a key new driver of Singapore's economic growth, and as outlined by Goh, this would be a sector which the authorities wanted and needed private companies to join hands with the government. The young Kwek was immediately intrigued. "Lee Kuan Yew and Goh Keng Swee were supermen, you know?" he said. "They wanted to promote Singapore and to make the country alive and vibrant. I was very confident that tourism would take off."

He would find his opening into the sector quickly. By 1967, the efforts of Goh had paid off. In the first half of the year, some 87,000 tourists visited Singapore, a 57 per cent increase. An STPB spokesman called it a "world record." But the country had a major problem. It did not have enough hotels to meet this demand. An airline official told the media that this phenomenal rate of increase could not be maintained unless there was a massive acceleration in the number of rooms for tourists. "At present, the shortage has not only driven some tourists to seek accommodation in Johor Bahru, but also prompted certain overseas tour operators to advise potential tourists to skip Singapore in their itinerary," said the unnamed official.

The government made land in Havelock Road, by the banks of the Singapore River, available for new hotels to be built. The concentration of hotels along the Orchard Road shopping belt was no longer sufficient to meet the rising demand. To draw greater demand to build hotels, the authorities offered an attractive 10-year instalment plan, interest-free. Kwek was keen, saying in 2004 that he used to "pine for the day when I would own a hotel." And with it, Hong Leong found the opportunity to enter its fourth industry after building materials, finance and property — hotels. "Once there was this commitment to grow tourism, you can never go wrong to be involved in hotels," said Kwek. "Hotels would also give good recurring income." Hong Leong won a tender in 1968 and built its first hotel with a land cost of only S$980,000 in Havelock. Today, the land value is estimated at S$160 million.

In 1970, King's Hotel opened as part of a "build, build, build mania" in the local hotel industry, said *The Straits Times*. "It was first spurred on by the coming of the jumbo and supersonic age, lest we are caught napping as the crowds come crashing in." While fellow newbies like the Shangri-La, the Hyatt and the Mandarin along Orchard Road strove for the top-end tourist dollars, Kwek and Hong Leong positioned King's as a tourist-class hotel with 175 rooms. "It aims at attracting the middle-income tourists," wrote *The Straits Times* at its opening, as the 12-storey hotel drew attention with its graceful white façade and rounded balconies. To complement the new S$4.7-million hotel, the owners of ugly godowns in the area even agreed to give their buildings a facelift. "Scaffolding is now up and walls of the godowns are being given a new coat of paint so that patrons of the hotel will have a better view to look at," said Kwek to the *Eastern Sun* newspaper in 1970. "The godowns' owners' gesture of goodwill and cooperation is very much appreciated."

Business was brisk. But Kwek was an anxious young hotel owner. The hotel's long-time general manager Yeoh Cheng Kung said that Kwek would park himself at the hotel lobby almost every night in its early years, literally watching the business. He had gotten married in that same year, and his wife Cecilia recalled many a night of their early years as a married couple spent at King's lobby. "I would be drinking hot chocolate and he would be walking round and round to see who checked in," she said with a laugh.

Kwek would go through the books daily, mingled with the guests for feedback, and even booked a room "incognito" to observe his staff at work. Kwek said: "Every night, after dinner, I would head down to the hotel and sit at the lobby. When I saw guests arriving, I would clap in delight and be most happy! But when no one was coming, I would be dismayed. I'll ask: 'Where are the guests? Why are they not coming? What rates are we charging? Are we driving away the guests?' I was very hands-on and that has remained so up till today."

Senior staff in Millennium & Copthorne Hotels now said that Kwek had two standard questions when he reached any one of his hotels: What's the occupancy? What's the average room rate last night? They were habits honed from his nights spent at the lobby of King's, said Yeoh. "He used King's Hotel as his base and as the place for him to learn about the hotel business," he shared. "He was very demanding for profits and would push you very hard to do something to improve the bottom line." In a popular anecdote shared in the hotel group today, a hotel general manager excitedly told the visiting Kwek that his establishment had 99 per cent occupancy that day. Kwek replied: "Why not 100?"

While business was good in King's, margins were thin. Kwek soon realised that at 175 rooms, the hotel lacked a critical mass. He obtained permission from the authorities to build a new tower with 142 additional rooms. "I told the government that we were all new to this hotel business. You didn't know, I didn't know, we all made mistakes — 175 rooms were not enough. Let me build a new tower," said Kwek. "They said that if they allowed me, they would have to do the same to my neighbours — Apollo and Miramar. I said give it to them too! You want to make tourism viable in Singapore? They eventually agreed."

The expansion put King's on a firm footing and despite navigating numerous crises including the SARS epidemic in 2003 and the COVID-19 pandemic from 2020 to 2022, the hotel has never been in the red for more than 50 years, shared Yeoh proudly. Kwek had positioned the hotel correctly, tapping on a wide pool of cost-conscious travellers. "A lot of people think that five-star hotels are the best, but actually three-star hotels are more profitable," he said. "The cost is much lower and so you enjoy better margins than luxury hotels."

Kwek tapped on Hong Leong's strong relations with Japanese businessmen to grow King's in its early years, employing not only a Japanese general manager to run the place, but also setting up a Japanese restaurant and a Japanese barber shop — ideas which were fairly unheard of in Singapore in the 1970s. The hotel succeeded in drawing regular visitors and flight crew from Japan, and even celebrities like British pop singer Engelbert Humperdinck.

The hotel's creativity and flexibility also helped it to stay in the black for half a century. For starters, Kwek wanted the hotel to serve more than tourists. He correctly predicted in the early 1970s that Singapore was on the cusp of massive economic development and with it, the growth of a nascent middle class. These Singaporeans with some means would want to pamper themselves every now and then, and he marketed King's as a choice venue for local rendezvous — not quite as expensive as the luxurious hotels along Orchard Road, but certainly a clear upgrade from the street hawkers of the era. At a time when Western food was still the norm in hotel coffee houses in Singapore, King's bucked the trend to offer authentic Penang Nonya cuisine. The buffet spread remains a local favourite today after 50 years.

All these early lessons, challenges and successes at King's would translate into Kwek's hotel modus operandi later. His hands-on style gave rise to a flat management structure across his global empire, minimising bureaucracy and giving managers the autonomy to make quick decisions on room rates, promotions and food and beverage changes. And in a move straight out of the King's playbook, Kwek managed to get rare planning permission in the 1990s from the

London authorities to expand his Bailey's Hotel. It was an upgrade which British analysts described as a "godsend."

Kwek also made British hotels look at food and beverage differently, said the Gloucester's general manager Grant Wilkins in 1995. Chinese congee and American eggs benedict were added to the breakfast buffets, forcing London staid competitors to catch up. "We now look at our F&B outlets in a more creative way, very much as the hotels in South-east Asia look at them," he said in an interview with *The Business Times*. "We no longer operate like a typical European hotel where you have a coffee-shop and an a-la-carte restaurant. We now have niche restaurants for markets that we believe will be attracted to them both internally and externally." A noted London travel industry leader described Kwek's impact on Britain's hotels as enormous.

The Singaporean also never forgot his love of hanging out at King's lobby. He never orders room service when he stays in his hotels overseas, preferring to spend time at or near the lobbies to get a better feel of operations. "He wants to see people, watch business, find out what kind of clientele," observed a senior staff. It would explain why while the man would move on to far more glamorous and trendy hotels, the humble King's — now known as Copthorne King's Hotel — remained the one he loved dearest. As he said more than once in interviews, he learnt and finessed many of his hotel management styles and techniques there in the lobby of the humble hotel across the road from the Singapore River.

He admitted that it is the only establishment in his portfolio which is not for sale — regardless of the price. "This is my first hotel and I learnt a lot from it. Why would I want to sell it? There are some assets which are not for sale," he said, stressing that his successors know that King's must always remain in the hands of the Kweks. His wife even nicknamed it their family business' "mother hotel" which should not be altered or changed unnecessarily.

Although he is not a superstitious man, there are hints that he believed King's had brought him good fortune, said Yeoh. "King's Hotel was his baby, and it grew up to be the mother of his hotel empire, the place where it all began. How can you sell your mother? King's Hotel has been auspicious to him," said Yeoh. Kwek suggested as much. When asked why he chose the name for the hotel, he replied with a glint in his eyes: "Because I knew I would be the king of hotels."

Chapter 6

In the Name of the Father

"My father had a significant impact on me. He had been my mentor. There is much about this business I learnt from him that no business school can teach me."

— Kwek Leng Beng in a speech in 2002.

When the news came in August 1990, Kwek Leng Beng was braced for impact. After a lengthy trial involving Queen's Counsels and a billionaire in the dock, the verdict was a painful one to accept. His father, Kwek Hong Png, and a cousin were each fined S$5,000 after pleading guilty to a breach of the Companies Act. They had been accused of not using due diligence in discharging their duties as directors of Tripartite Developers, a real estate company largely owned by Hong Leong Holdings. Both had improperly authorised Tripartite to pay a real estate broking firm, and were fined.

As a result, both men were barred for five years from holding directorships or participating in the management of companies. It meant Kwek Hong Png had to step down as chairman of City

Developments (CDL) and the Hong Leong Group. His son Leng Beng, who was about to turn 50, had already assumed leadership of Hong Leong Finance in 1984, but now it was time for him to step up completely. "I was as ready as ever," he said. "It had been a journey where I learnt as much as I could from him." He was flanked and supported by his younger brother Leng Joo, who became the managing director of CDL.

In the years since, Kwek has gradually distilled the lessons from his father into 10 key takeaways which have guided his business thinking and decisions over the next three decades.

▶ Be pragmatic

Ideologies work beautifully in ivory towers, but for Kwek Hong Png, there was no place for dogma in the business world. If there was one philosophy he clung on to fiercely, it was to do whatever that works. Love and hate, and likes and dislikes were irrelevant. How he treated the Japanese was instructive. While his first wife died during the Japanese Occupation and he was once beaten up by the occupiers, it did not stop him from working with them to first make a living and later to build a fortune.

Kwek Leng Beng recalled his father saying: "He said business is business. Differences with the Japanese is another matter. While he had suffered under them during the war, it didn't mean he did not want to do business with them. He was a practical and pragmatic man. He would do what he thought was right without any fear."

This ability to set aside his emotions continued into the post-war years. Hong Leong's major breakthroughs came with joint ventures with major Japanese industrialists. Their ties remain till today. When Hong Leong completed its own 45-storey building in 1977, most of the tenants were Japanese companies. King's Hotel's major clientele in its early days were Japanese businessmen and flight crew.

▶ Know the world

Kwek Hong Png had two big convictions which he used as the foundations of his major business decisions. First, he believed the Japanese would not be able to win the war and remain for long. That gave him the confidence to invest heavily even during the war years, buying properties and rubber plantations.

Second, he saw that the new People's Action Party government in Singapore was on the right track and would be not only a pro-people's party — as its name implies — but also a pro-business one. "In my view, the government policies have always been in support of business," he said in *Leaders of Singapore*. "The government must have policies which are good for businessmen, then it will succeed in attracting investment from foreigners and local investors. Then the economy can develop and there will be economic growth."

These over-the-horizon kind of perspectives outlined global and local megatrends which companies today pay millions to management consultants for. Kwek Leng Beng followed his old man's focus on knowing the world. He always made it a point to keep abreast of the latest news, said his nephew Kevin Hangchi, who is the senior vice-president of Hong Leong Management Services. "He would have read everything in the newspapers by the time he started work each morning," he said. "Not a simple task as his subscriptions included overseas newspapers as well. Not only would he read widely, but he also made it a point to find out what was happening around him."

That's not enough. Kwek also wants "street intelligence" and demands that his employees find out what is happening in their world. It is a hands-on investigative process which he likes to call "*tum tia*" in Hokkien. "In this way he always had his finger on the pulse of the group's businesses and with his ear to the ground for the latest market news and opportunities to drive profits," added Hangchi.

It pays to understand politics, and also help influence policies. Critically, Kwek learnt from his father the importance of helping to build not only your own company, but also the larger society and economy, said fellow real estate businessman Philip Ng, son of property mogul Ng Teng Fong. "We are not just business people in Singapore per se. We are also participating in the national development and economic growth of Singapore. That's how our fathers saw it, and that's how LB saw it, and I respect him for thinking about the industry and the country."

▶ Land is wealth

Once the long-term roadmap has been established, it allows businesses to think in years and maybe even decades, rather than quarters or months. For Kwek Hong Png, that meant a licence to invest, and his favourite is land. "I believe that land is the most secure foundation in business," he wrote in his autobiography. "Where there is land, there is wealth, and wealth opens many avenues. Or as the old saying goes: the soil can yield white jade, the land can yield gold."

Even when he was a near penniless migrant worker, he dreamt of investing in land. "It has always been my ambition to acquire land and develop property," he wrote. "Even as an apprentice, I had often looked at the shophouses lining the banks of the Singapore River and imagined my own towering building in their midst." This lesson was so well-drilled into his son that Kwek Leng Beng would stress that "land is gold" in every interview conducted for this book.

▶ Taking risks

Once your fundamentals of being pragmatic and knowing the world have been established, businessmen cannot be too cautious and careful. Kwek Hong Png dared to take risks during a war, spotting opportunities and seizing them. In no time, Hong Leong had outgrown his brother-in-law's business, which remained conservative and overly careful.

It was also a major bugbear which Kwek had of his son, especially in his early years in the family business. But the scion had clearly learnt well. In a speech in 2002, he said: "I want to share with you this anecdote about a former employee of our company. I had known him since childhood. He was always smarter than I was. When he asked for an opening in the company, I offered him one. He was assigned to the loans department to bring in loans for the company.

"While many would take three months to learn the ropes, he did it in under a week. When he was tested on his knowledge and theory, he passed with flying colours. Nine months into his job, I found out that he had not approved a loan to anyone. When I questioned him, he said: 'What if he died of a heart attack? What if he met with an accident? What if he quarrelled with his wife? Then the loans wouldn't be repaid.' This episode highlights that he was not even willing to take calculated risks. To survive in a business environment, you have to be practical and pragmatic and not be too theoretical."

▶ Cash flow is king

Clearly, Kwek Hong Png was not an advocate of wild risk taking. He emphasised the importance of cash flow in business, and to minimise borrowing unless there is an objective to be achieved. In 1948, he wrote, Hong Leong could have obtained bank credits of 10 to 15 times its then paid-up capital of $300,000 to fund its growth. "However we chose to keep our borrowing to a minimum by relying more on our own resources," he wrote.

Kwek Leng Beng said that sometimes he could still hear his father's caution to not over-leverage. "I remember he used to tell me: 'When you don't have cash flow coming in, you have outflow, you will be a bankrupt, better be careful'," he recalled. "With any business, there are always expenses to be considered. Without cash flow, no business can survive, no matter how good the product or how talented its management may be," he said in an interview with *Tatler* magazine in 2018.

While expansion is in itself a desired outcome, it has to be balanced with cash level. "You have to know when to stop (expansion)," he said in 2002. "You cannot, like a punter, keep on piling up your bets hoping that every time you punt, you will strike it big. In most cases, many expand too fast to the point that they end up going bust. There are two things that need to be addressed with regards to expansion. First, you have to know when to stop as well as when to retreat. The second is over-gearing. Many expand with excessive borrowing. If their business hits a snag, their operations would be hampered with a large mountain of debts."

▶ Managing costs

This is where thrift comes in. Kwek Hong Png stressed it as the "most important" lesson he had taught his brothers, sons and even grandsons. "Whatever we do, we have to have a plan. We cannot do things without planning. As for expenses, we must always try to be as thrifty as possible. But then if there are certain expenses to be spent, you must not cut cost," he said in his Oral History interview.

His son has imbibed this lesson completely. As former long-time Hong Leong Finance employee James Sim shared: "Kwek Leng Beng would go through your expenses and make sure they are claimed accurately. He would compensate you fairly, but not more." Kwek liked to share the story of Motel 6 as a cautionary tale of how poor management of costs can lead to serious problems. Even though the American chain was making good profits in the budget hotels sector in the 1970s and 1980s, the management failed to keep tabs on theft by staff emptying the cash registers. "Despite good sales, because of poor cost control the company could not sustain the business and had to dispose of it," he shared in 2002, adding: "Keeping track of your costs and trimming them when necessary is important in any business. However, you can cut your costs only to a certain point. At some point, you have to start again focusing on your sales. In a nutshell, it is sales that finally determine the fate and fortune of a business or a company."

▶ No zero-sum game

Kwek Hong Png eschewed a zero-sum game and was always looking to secure win-win solutions, said his son. "One of the most important values he stressed was to be fair and above board in your conduct," he shared. "There is no winner-takes-all mentality or attitude." Just like how he shared ownership of Hong Leong with his three brothers, Kwek Hong Png believed in doing business in a manner which benefits all parties, rather than a beggar-thy-neighbour approach. Asked what were his best moments in business, he replied: "The most memorable times are spent together with my closest business associates."

Kwek Leng Beng kept his lesson in mind, said fellow real estate tycoon Philip Ng. "He doesn't speak up on only personal issues related to CDL and Hong Leong," he observed through years of working together in the Real Estate Developers' Association of Singapore. "He has a heart for the real estate sector. We don't look at ourselves as real rivals, because we see that we are all in the same boat on this small island. And we all have a place."

This lack of rivalry was evident in Kwek's global affairs too, said former Hilton group CEO David Michels. In the early 2000s, Hilton signed on to manage another hotel in Seoul, breaking an exclusive agreement it had with Kwek as operator of the Seoul Hilton. Kwek asked to meet London-based Michels. "He suggested we met halfway," said Michels. "Halfway for Leng Beng was Bangkok. So I flew to Bangkok. We had a serious argument amongst friends."

Kwek pressed Hilton for compensation and obtained an undisclosed sum. "I said 'Look, Leng Beng, I'm going to fly back to London and this is a big personal embarrassment for me. What can you do to help me?' He said 'I just bought a half-finished hotel in Bangkok. Hilton can have this on a 10-year management contract.' So I lost a few millions and gained US$20 million. So we turned a very fierce argument into a very good solution for both companies. That wasn't me being clever. That was Leng Beng being clever. Was it calculated? Probably not. But that's Leng Beng for you, very smart. He wanted it to be a Hilton anyhow and it was right for Hilton." The hotel remains a Hilton, under Kwek's ownership, today. "He has a big hammer, but he doesn't always use it," added Michels. No zero-sum games.

▶ Build reputation

It followed that he sought to build good long-term relations in the business world, rather than attempt to gain a quick buck. From suppliers to clients, Hong Leong came to be known as a trustworthy brand which does not cut corners. As Kwek Leng Beng said, his father wanted to establish a reputation in the market. "It wasn't just to make money, make money and make more money," he said.

So while developers in the 1980s raced to the bottom to fatten margins and sacrifice quality, CDL bucked the trend. "It was easy to not care about quality and leave it to the buyers," he said. "But we were not in a hurry to sell, sell, sell. If you don't have good quality, your reputation would always be stained. We were thinking long term; we wanted our business to be sustainable."

Till today, CDL staff said that Kwek frequently stressed the importance of protecting the company's reputation. "He is a decent business person," said a long-time senior aide. "He has never come from an angle to take advantage of others. A lot of business people will seize any opportunity at all costs. He will never do that. He always talked about being fair and equitable."

It is an observation shared by W. Chan Kim, one of the world's top management thinkers. "I have known Chairman Kwek for more than 20 years. He is a very honest man with high integrity," said the INSEAD professor behind the famous Blue Ocean strategy. "He says what he means and he delivers on his promises. It's quite rare in the global business world."

Indeed, when asked about his legacy in a media interview in 2018, Kwek Leng Beng did not point to a particular business deal or a breathtaking building he had made possible. Instead, he said he would like to be known for being a fair person. "What can be sustainable over time should be the measure of success. I would like to think that the legacy I leave behind will be the decency in all my dealings while remaining truthful to my objectives and focus as a business person," he said. "Never taking advantage of others when doing business and do so with integrity. Do business fair and square and leave some margins for people, so that they have trust and faith to deal with you again and again. Be responsible and keep my word."

▶ Familiarity breeds prosperity

Kwek Hong Png stressed to his successor to do the business they were familiar with and not stray unnecessarily into whatever that could have been popular or in vogue. "He said that if you do things which you do not know, you could get swallowed up," said Kwek Leng Beng. So while conglomerates, especially in places likes South Korea and Indonesia, extend into a mind-wandering array of businesses, the Hong Leong Group has thus followed a fairly linear and logical pattern of diversification. It began with building materials, before moving into the connected sectors of real estate, finance and hotels. "I prefer to be a specialist," he said.

Such familiarity allows for greater domain knowledge, which the Kweks believe is critical to success and prosperity. "It literally means dirtying your hands and getting to know your business first-hand. There is simply no substitute for this," said Kwek Leng Beng. He is known to make quiet checks on both potential investments and existing assets. Overseas, he would travel with only one aide to survey new hotels incognito. At home, he slips into his hotels early in the morning unannounced, said former CDL director Eric Chan. "He doesn't rely only on regular updates from his staff. He will try to confirm that what was put up to him is true," shared Chan. "For example, if they tell him that a restaurant's food is good but yet the business is not so good, then he will quietly try to find out what the problem might be. Is it the marketing, is it the pricing, or even the signage? While he has very high demands on his staff to do the work, he will also roll up his sleeves and do the work himself."

This hands-on approach extends beyond the nuts and bolts of the business, shared Kwek. "Your knowledge of the business should expand to incorporate the economic climate you are operating in as well as legislations that could impact your growth. Being mindful of these areas would enable you to make sound and rational decisions."

The knowledge will sharpen business acumen and judgment, leading to better decisions. Do not follow the crowd, be it the dotcom craze or the bubble tea fad, said Kwek. "Unless your new business complements your existing one, moving into an entirely new product or service is not a strategic move," he said in 2002. "Always bear in mind that an entirely new business has its own inherent risks. Being a newcomer, you may not have the ability to identify these risks. When you miss out on these, it would be difficult for you to make the new business work. The end result is: your existing business too will suffer."

▶ Passion

For all the above to work, the last and secret ingredient is passion. Kwek Hong Png lived for his business. He said in *Leaders*: "Doing business is my hobby! I have little time for other activities." His son wholeheartedly followed in his father's footsteps. He professed to have little patience for socialising outside of business-related events. And just like his father, his hobby was his business. "Doing business has been and still is my passion. I believe that if you're not passionate, at best you can be mediocre," he said in the *Tatler* interview. "If you have the knowledge, the experiences and the passion, but do not contribute or pass to others, that would be such a waste."

In advice he shared with other business leaders in 2002, he said: "Always be passionate about the business you are in. It would be suicidal to go into a business that you have no love or interest in. For example, if you have no interest in tennis and you are asked to learn to play tennis, you will never learn to play it well, even if an experienced coach tutors you. On the other hand, if you are passionate about the game, there is no telling what you would do to become an expert. You will read books and magazines about how to play tennis. You will try to emulate the strokes by watching countless hours of videos of top tennis players. You will undertake all these because it is the passion for the game that drives you. It's the same with any business. Be passion-driven."

He is always thinking about work and is notorious in the business world for being allergic to small talk. The first time he met Daniel Desbaillets at the opening of the InterContinental Singapore, the first thing he asked the Swiss head of the new hotel was: "How much was the building cost? What are your projections, occupancy, average rate going forward? You've got so many hotels next to you, how are you going to compete with them?" Forget about pleasantries, it's a waste of time. Former Singapore Cabinet Minister George Yeo concurred. He said: "I've always found him to be serious, never satisfied, never happy. Always worrying, always concerned, always hoping that things could be better. That's always been my impression of Leng Beng, always with a frown. Never one for small talk, very focused on the business."

Fellow property mogul Philip Ng of Far East Organization joked that Kwek does a bit of small talk with those he is very familiar with. "Maybe 5 to 10 per cent," he said with a laugh. "He told me he was very afraid of meeting my father because my father always gave him such bad food. My father loved chicken rice and curry and would take LB to Far East Plaza for lunch. LB didn't like it — he found it quite oily. He said the food was terrible, better not meet in Far East Plaza. Between us there's a little bit of small talk. He's quite cute."

The passion will lead to hard work, a necessary ingredient for success, said Kwek. He worked 12-hour days six days a week for most of his career, and even tossed in a few hours on Sundays. "You have to put in lots of time nurturing and cultivating your business. This is sometimes even at the expense of your family and social life." His wife shared that he rarely went on family vacations. His son Sherman recalled that his father was seldom around when he was young.

It is a sacrifice which successful entrepreneurs must be prepared for. Kwek professed to having very few friends, a loneliness which fellow Singapore-based businessman Ron Sim — a business contact — said he could identify with. "Both he and I are very much focused on our businesses. I have very few close friends too," he shared. "True leaders are like eagles; you have to fly alone."

It is worth it if you love it, said Kwek. "There are some who, despite all their hard work and drudgery, love what they do. This is because they view work as a hobby. To put it simply, work hard, talk less and do more."

Four years after founder Kwek Hong Png stepped down as chairman, he passed away in 1994. For his son and successor, there was a sharp awareness that the heavy load of carrying, and growing, this family enterprise had landed on him for the rest of his life, said his wife Cecilia. "He knew that the burden had started," she said. "Whatever little time he had with me, it would be gone. From then on, my life would be different. It would be more lonely."

Kwek Leng Beng had lost his mentor and tormentor, opening up a hole in his life which would only widen as he ages. "Today, he really misses his father," said Cecilia. "Now he knows why the father was so harsh — it was to educate him. After his father passed away, he has tried very hard to figure out what the old man said. He tries to adopt the same principles."

"

One of the most important values (my father) stressed was to be fair and above board in your conduct. There is no winner-takes-all mentality or attitude.

— Kwek Leng Beng

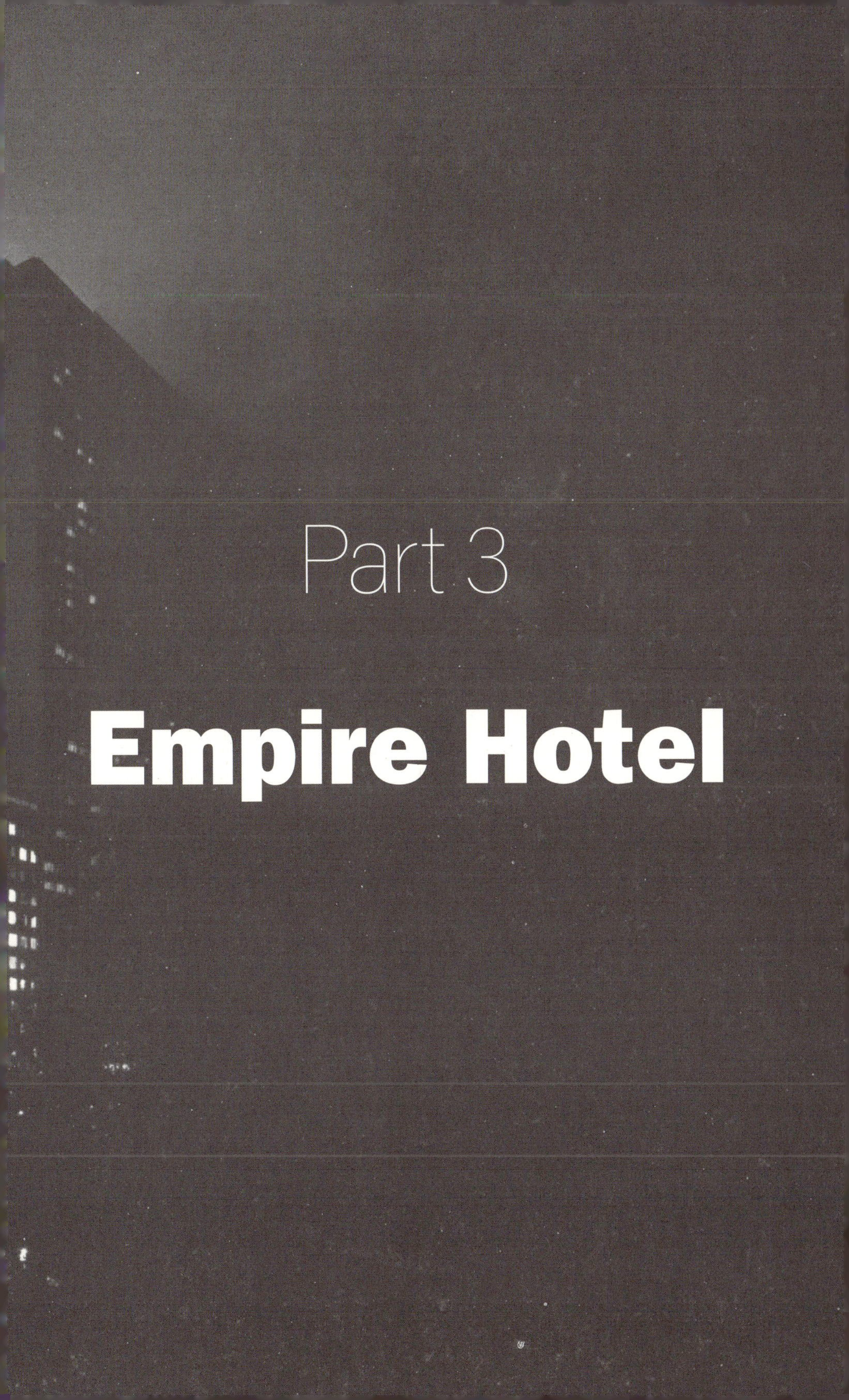

Part 3

Empire Hotel

”

I knew I would be the king of hotels.

— Kwek Leng Beng

CHAPTER 7

From King's to Kingdom

"His ambition is to create the first global hotel brand to come out of Asia."

— Forbes *magazine on Kwek Leng Beng in 2001.*

When Kwek Leng Beng took over from his father in the early 1990s, the business and the world stood at the crossroads of revolution, reform and reorganisation. The Cold War was hobbling to an end after the fall of the Berlin Wall, and the repercussions to this purported end of history swept the world from west to east. There was a bloody crackdown in Beijing which came to be known as the Tiananmen Incident of 1989. Closer to home in South-east Asia, Vietnam pulled out of Cambodia after 11 years of a bloody occupation. After decades of turbulence, the region which Kwek called home would finally find some peace.

When a United States-led coalition steamrollered into Kuwait in response to the Iraqi invasion in 1990, it was heralded as the beginning not only of a new decade — and the last one of the 20th century — but also of a new unipolar age of development and prosperity. Change was afoot in Singapore too, as the tiny island nation saw its first leadership transition since independence, from founding Prime Minister Lee Kuan Yew to Goh Chok Tong. Whether it was a pledge to build a "kinder and gentler" society, or an election campaign slogan of "More Good Years," the new Goh administration stood for a promise of better times and better lives.

The geopolitical changes of the world and at home would dovetail perfectly with Kwek ascending to the top of his family business empire. Just as Goh wanted to leave his own imprimatur on the country, Kwek was similarly driven to carve a new niche for himself and by extension Hong Leong. He would find it in the posh and glamorous world of hotels.

In 1989, shortly before the elder Kwek moved away from the frontlines, the Hong Leong Group made a strategic decision to add hotel ownership and management to its property, finance and building materials conglomerate in a big way. Part of reason was because of its inability to get the much-cherished banking licence from the Singapore government. But the new venture would be the perfect platform for Kwek to build his own name in the most colourful, and at times dramatic, fashion.

As *The Business Times* columnist Conrad Raj noted in 2000: "For years, Kwek Leng Beng had struggled to come out from under the shadow of his father, legendary property magnate Kwek Hong Png. And while his more flamboyant cousin Quek Leng Chan was regarded as a more aggressive and entrepreneurial businessman, he was considered dull and unexciting."

Not anymore. Kwek would parlay his experience building and managing King's Hotel into one of the world's biggest hotel kingdoms, said former CDL director Foo See Juan. "He was the architect behind the hotel expansion," he said. "He was very passionate about hotels and single-handedly turned CDL into a truly global player."

When he began on his conquest, he had only six hotels under his charge, all of them in Asia:

- King's Hotel (Singapore)
- Orchid Inn (Singapore)
- Orchard Hotel (Singapore)
- Grand Hyatt Taipei (Taiwan)
- Manila Plaza Hotel (The Philippines)
- Orchid Hotel Penang (Malaysia)

The hotels were consolidated under a new subsidiary called City Developments Limited Hotels, or CDL Hotels, and listed in Hong Kong in 1989. City Developments held 51 per cent stake in the entity, which enjoyed an initial market capitalisation of HK$3 billion. Armed with this war chest, Kwek went shopping for hotels. He had five basic principles.

▶ The price must be right

Unlike the Japanese who rushed into the United States and bought trophy properties in the 1980s at record prices, the Singaporean did not follow the crowd. "My father said to me: 'You must buy at the right time, at the right price'," he recalled. "If you go in and just buy, buy, buy...that's not the strategy." In 1992, the London hotel market was in such doldrums that no major hotel had not been sold since 1989. Kwek would take the opportunity to buy the 548-room Gloucester for US$109 million. In an interview with the *Wall Street Journal* in 1997, he said: "I didn't believe in going to the West when everyone else was rushing there. I went when everyone else was running away. If sellers start asking (for) too much money, I'm just not going to buy."

The world took note of his ability to sniff out bargains repeatedly. In 1995, the *New York Times* said that his company "has an impressive record of paying relatively little for profitable hotels in Singapore, Britain, New Zealand, the United States and elsewhere." Forbes praised Kwek for having "dispassionate buyer's discipline," always prepared to walk away when the price is not right. It was most notable in Japan, a country which he was scouting for years but never found the right moment with the right price. In the aftermath of the Fukushima nuclear disaster in 2011, land prices nosedived and he acquired prime land in Ginza shopping district in the heart of Tokyo. "I have witnessed the birth of a hotel in a country that is difficult for foreigners to invest in," he said with much pride at the opening of the Millennium Mitsui Garden Hotel in 2014.

Sir David Michels, the former chief executive of the Hilton

group, said that Kwek is known in the industry for being unemotional about his hotels. "I don't think he loves this one because it's blue, or this one because it's pink, or this one because he got married there. A lot of hoteliers do, by the way."

Location, location, location

Kwek wanted the best locations in the best cities around the world: London, New York, Hong Kong. In 1992, he bought the Nikko Hotel Hong Kong in the bustling tourist and nightlife district of Tsim Sha Tsui in southern Kowloon. Similarly, the Gloucester sits in the affluent Kensington district of London, home to Imperial College London, the Royal Albert Hall and upmarket shops. It is also where Kensington Palace, home of the Prince and Princess of Wales, is located. "It's all about the location," he stressed. His eye for prime location is unparalleled, shared his Middle East partner Ali Al Zaabi, who now operates about 50 hotels under the Millennium & Copthorne brand. "Look at his Biltmore Mayfair in London," he said. "This is a location which cannot be replicated. Everybody knows Mayfair. When no one was buying, he went in."

To get the best insights in an unfamiliar territory, he often turned to local taxi drivers, shared Kwek. One of his favourite hotel hunting tactics is to ditch the chauffeured limousine and grab a taxi, at times on his own. He did that in Barcelona in 2019 before turning down a purchase, and likewise in Liverpool in

2015 when he bought The Beatles-inspired Hard Days Night Hotel. He would strike up a conversation with the cabbie on the way to the targeted hotel, and attempt to find out as much as possible. Is this a good part of the town? Are there tidbits and taboos of the location which only the locals would know? Chances are, the hotel he had in mind would be a distressed property. What caused the place to fall on hard times? Would a change of ownership and management make a difference? He wanted true local unvarnished views. As always, he gets on the ground. "Hotels are not something you do on your phone or computer," said Al Zaabi.

▶ Tenure of a property

Buying a hotel is as much about the building as the land it sits on. For Kwek, who had been in the property business for two decades by 1990, he paid primary attention to the land. To be specific, the tenure of a property. And his preference could be summed up in one word: "Freehold." The outright ownership of the land with no time limit speaks to the heart of a man who looked beyond the far horizon in his business decisions. Kwek was not a speculator.

He explained: "In this world, leasehold does not last long. You have to go and renew the lease. And freehold is always more valuable than leasehold. That's what I learned from my late father. He said, 'Land is gold.' When you have gold, there are plenty of safeguards. When you have safeguards, nobody can rob you of the gold." It applies even today. But he acknowledged that while he still prefers freehold today, they may not necessarily be available. For this reason, when he was given three hotels in London to choose from in 1992, two of which were on leasehold land, he chose the Gloucester which sat on freehold land.

▶ Profitability

Even when the price was cheap and the location was fantastic, Kwek would turn away if the yield was not good. As he told *Journal*: "Some people buy a hotel that is operating at a loss with the hope of turning it around. We don't believe in that." Instead, he was stubbornly disciplined with the hotel deals that came his way. "It can be very cheap, but if it has no cash flow, it's no good." If the first-year yield was not at least 10 per cent of the purchase price, before debts were taken into account, and he saw little room to improve, he would reject the offer. As his then financial adviser Simon Cheong said to the *Journal*: "Forget the bricks and mortar. His famous question is, 'What's the gross operating profit?'"

Kwek injected real estate sensibilities into the hotel business, said veteran hotelier Daniel Desbaillets, a former president with InterContinental Asia Pacific. "He looked at the profitability of a hotel from a per square footage angle," he shared. "Every square foot of a building must have an income. So, for example, the lobby of a hotel takes up a lot of space. It conveys opulence, makes a statement as a brand, but it doesn't really create revenue. He was probably among the first to have smaller lobbies and limited space where there was no revenue generating index."

When Kwek renovated his Orchard Hotel in Singapore, he slashed the size of the lobby and gave the space to food and beverage outlets. "There's this element for him that everything has a dollar and cent value," added Desbaillets. "We don't really gear to every dollar and cent in this fashion in Europe. He has utilised his entrepreneurship of a real estate tycoon in a hotel. Not many hotel companies do that."

▶ Hotel management

While Kwek was muscling into the hotel business as an owner, he was not yet a manager of hotels in a big way. In those early days, his CDL Hotels had yet to create their own management brands, the likes of Marriotts and Holiday Inns. He had that ambition, saying: "Our vision is to create a chain like Hilton, Sheraton or Hyatt." So to ensure what he bought could quickly turn profitable, one of his rules was to ensure that the hotel purchased came with a management contract. Industry experts referred to CDL as investors more than hoteliers at this point. "They identified the hotel market as attractive and underpriced, but outsiders run their properties," said Douglas P. Hercher, a director of real estate firm Jones Lang Wootton USA, in 1995 in the *New York Times*.

Kwek wanted to build his hotel empire in the shortest amount of time. He was not a patient man. Instead of building hotels, he bought aggressively so as to bring immediate cash flow. "It's better and cheaper to buy into existing hotels, especially when they are yielding a positive cashflow," he told *The Business Times* in 2000. He started with the Gloucester in London in late 1992, stunning the hotel world. "Everyone thought he was crazy," an unnamed investment adviser said in the *Journal*. The deal "was way out in front of the curve, in terms of buying a good asset at a time when everyone thought the market was trashed forever."

It was followed two months later with the Nikko Hotel purchase in Hong Kong, and then another month later with the Regent Hotel in Kuala Lumpur, Malaysia. In four short months, by taking advantage of the depressed market conditions around the world, Kwek had increased his number of hotels by 50 per cent. He was not looking at any particular markets. As he told the *Journal*: "My father believed in Asia. I believe in the world-markets." By mid-1993, he had inked a deal with the consultancy of Singapore's former Deputy Prime Minister Goh Keng Swee to go into hotels in China. Goh was an adviser to the Chinese government in its reform and opening up policy.

The breakneck pace of expansion was unheard of. Hardly a month went by in 1993 without some news of a new hotel added to CDL Hotels' portfolio. Kwek was gobbling up hotels like a famished developer, and by July 1993, he was no longer content with a single bite. He wanted a big buffet spread, and he found it in the rather unsexy market Down Under in New Zealand.

CDL Hotels acquired 70 per cent of QINZ Holdings, taking a majority stake in the largest hotel chain in the country. QINZ is the holding company of the Quality Hotels in New Zealand, a chain of travellers' lodges. "The owner was desperate to offload, and I was curious," he said. "I asked him a lot of questions about his hotels and New Zealand and I decided to go take a look. People laughed at me. They said the country has more sheep than people, who would stay in your hotels?" It helped that all the land which the Quality Hotels sat on were freehold. Kwek sealed the deal quickly.

A month later, he expanded in New Zealand by acquiring Kingsgate International's five hotels and several parcels of land in key tourism areas. In the same month, he bought another hotel and began to build another one. In just two years, CDL Hotels had become the largest hotel operator in New Zealand with 20 hotels and 2,598 rooms. A Singapore tabloid remarked in 1995 that Kwek was buying hotels like "veggies at the market."

Kwek was hardly dogmatic, or vain, about the hotels he was buying. In an interview in 2014, he shared: "I once asked my late father, 'Why don't we position ourselves as a deluxe developer?' He said, 'Why be so silly? You should do whatever that can make money — deluxe, middle, lower end — cast your net wider.' This is the right strategy. Some people focus on luxury only because they want to create a statement for themselves. But the trick is, a three-star makes more money than a four-star, a four-star more than a five-star. I choose to cast my net wider so I have better profits and spread my risk."

The pragmatic businessman was completely not hung up about status symbols, always focused on the bottom line and not the headlines. His hotel kingdom was taking shape across three continents — Asia, Oceania and Europe. It was an impressive feat coming from a small country, said fellow businessman Ron Sim. "He is a visionary entrepreneur and one of the very few from Singapore who have planted our flag around the world," he said.

Such worldwide acquisitions at a time when globalisation was only taking off as a buzzword was a "visionary move," praised fellow Singaporean real estate mogul Philip Ng. "It was quite deft moving into markets which were quite unfamiliar to the rest of us," he said. "He seemed to have a better grasp of it. There were some very good properties that he found and he invested in. The rest of us were totally unfamiliar with those markets. So we were just sticking to our knitting. I think he was bold and visionary." Kwek would soon train his guns on the world's No 1 economy and the only superpower, the United States.

Chapter 8

New York, New York

"They have no bureaucracy. They respond immediately if they like what they see."

***— The Millenium Hilton's managing director Susan G. Ricci on the CDL Hotels' buying strategy, in the* New York Times.**

Start spreading the news
I'm leaving today
I want to be a part of it
New York, New York

New York, New York. Everything about New York agreed with Kwek Leng Beng. He loved cities, eschewed the countryside. And no city comes bigger, brighter and bolder than the Big Apple, Gotham City, the Capital of the World. He thrived on speed, demanding results at a digital pace even though he belonged very much in the analogue age. The relentless pace of Wall Street, of Broadway, of Times Square synced with the inner rhythm of a man whose favourite answer when asked about a deadline was "yesterday." He obsessed about locations and there is no more prestigious zip code in the world than Manhattan. After all, few places could be identified globally by its phone number area code, unlike bygone days when 212 denoted a cool connection at the heart of it all.

These vagabond shoes
They are longing to stray
Right through the very heart of it
New York, New York

When Kwek started building his hotel kingdom in 1989, he wanted to anchor it in New York. "It will always be a financial centre," he said. "It may be more vibrant at times, and less vibrant at others. But I always feel that New York is a place where you need to be — at the right time, at the right price."

Coincidentally, in the same year, Arturo di Modica, a Sicilian-born New York artist, chose to unload a 11-foot-tall, 7,100-pound bronze statue of a charging bull outside the New York Stock Exchange. He did not seek any permits, simply dumped his piece of guerrilla art under a giant Christmas tree in Lower Manhattan, and left. The Charging Bull was created by the artist to symbolise the United States' resilience and ability to bounce back after the 1987 stock market crash. He wanted the sculpture to "encourage everybody to realise America's power."

How appropriate then that it would become the single most enduring image of New York in the mind of Kwek. "Whenever I think of New York City, the first image that comes to mind is the bull," he said. In his own ways, the Singaporean was inspired by di Modica to embrace and realise his own power in the United States.

I want to wake up in a city
That never sleeps
And find I'm king of the hill
Top of the heap

He had his eyes set on the Helmsley Palace Hotel in mid-town Manhattan, bearing the address of Madison Avenue. The hotel consists of a portion of the Villard Houses, 19th-century landmarks preserved by the local government. The hotel was once so popular that it reportedly had to reject King Charles, then the Prince of Wales, because all of the rooms were occupied. But troubles started to mount in 1990, and the hotel was placed in receivership after its owners, the Helmsleys, became mired in financial difficulties.

Kwek put in a bid of US$180 million in 1993, but was edged out by the Sultan of Brunei who bought the place for US$202 million. It would only be a minor hiccup to Kwek's ambitions to make himself top of the heap in Manhattan.

These small town blues
They are melting away
I'll make a brand new start of it
In old New York

The next year, in 1994, he would make his New York breakthrough with the sleek Millenium Hotel in downtown Manhattan, only a very short walk from the Charging Bull. Real estate mogul Peter Kalikow had intentionally misspelled the name of his creation, taking the artistic liberty of dropping an "n," so that it could stand out among the many hotels in New York. It failed horribly. Almost as soon as it opened in 1992, the owner was declared bankrupt, and the banks and brokers were actively looking for a buyer.

Thanks to Kwek's acquisitions in Europe, Asia and New Zealand, he suffered no small town blues despite calling a tiny island nation home. In the hotel world, he was already gaining a reputation as a serious buyer. "Because of our reputation, we have a lot of people knocking on our doors offering us a lot of things," he said in a media interview in 1996. "But we won't buy just to make up the numbers. It has to be thought through."

If I can make it there
I'll make it anywhere
It's up to you
New York, New York

The Millenium was a great deal — to Kwek, and perhaps only Kwek. Kalikow had spent US$210 million to buy it and it could be purchased — almost brand new — at less than half the price. At a time when buyers were few after the stock market crash of 1987,

Kwek was the darling of banks which had foreclosed the properties from their original developers or owners. About 50 bidders had looked at the hotel and decided to pass. It was a 561-room hotel with almost no business on weekends in a depressed downtown market, observed the *Wall Street Journal*.

Kwek saw something others did not. Downtown Manhattan had only two other hotels and if he could sign a major chain to operate it, it might work. After appointing Hilton, he grabbed the hotel at US$75 million, and immediately tasked the management to solve the moribund weekend occupancy in the financial district, where business travellers packed the weekdays but departed on Fridays. "We needed them to think about how to fill the void during this poor period," he said. "It had some success."

For good measure, Kwek being the stickler for proper rules — financial or language — changed the name to the correct "Millennium" spelling with double "n"s. Its latest name is the Millennium Downtown New York Hotel, rebranded in 2022. Kwek would also use the Millennium name as the brand for his global hotel empire, a timely choice as he moved his business into the new 21st century. He had finally made his mark in the city, and was ready to make it anywhere else.

New York, New York
I want to wake up in a city
That doesn't sleep
And find that I'm number one
Top of the list
Head of the heap
King of the hill

Right after his first success, Kwek would follow up quickly with his next win, moving up north to midtown Manhattan and the famous Times Square. A few months after acquiring the Millenium, he was offered another new hotel in New York, the Hotel Macklowe, which was named after its owner, a well-known real estate developer. The building was a "timeless beauty" in his words. The lobby was laid out in wood and black marble, contrasted with plush grey and black carpets. Harry Macklowe wanted a showpiece architecture fit to bear his name, and Kwek was quick to recognise its allure and value.

The hotel drew much acclaim from the American media when it opened in 1989. The *New York Times* praised it for having an "imposing sense of style" and cited architectural critic Paul Goldberger as hailing the new marvel as "New York's proudest monument to the art of the deal." A *Los Angeles Times* review described the hotel as having "all the luxuries of the major chain hotels but none of the tackiness."

But while Macklowe spent US$190 million to build his dream

palace, he defaulted on several millions of debt on his other properties and his prized new trophy was seized by the creditors a few years later. In October 1994, the five-year-old hotel was bought by Kwek at only US$96 million. It was a bargain buy for the Singaporean, who was not afraid to outbid his US rivals, said the *New York Times*. "They bid against a lot of American chains...and they came up higher every time," said Frank Dougherty, senior vice-president of consultancy Hospitality Valuation Services. As an unnamed hotelier told the Singapore's *The Business Times* in 1996: "This guy is the ultimate business-cycle bottom fisher." He was top of the list, head of the heap, king of the hill.

These little town blues
They've all melted away
I'm gonna make a brand new start of it
In old New York

A year after Hotel Macklowe was in the bag, Kwek visited his new purchase and stepped outside the building to admire his beautiful hotel. Like a consummate businessman, his eyes were distracted by a "For Sale" sign on the adjacent Newspaper Guild. It was a modest three-storey building, a dwarf to Hotel Macklowe, which is today known as the Millennium Broadway Times Square. Kwek was intrigued and asked for the price of the Newspaper Guild building. But he was told it had already been sold. "Oh, okay. It's all right, never mind," he said, and forgot about the matter.

Months later in 1996, on yet another trip to New York, Kwek saw that the "For Sale" sign was still on the tiny building. Surprised, he asked for an update: "Why is the sign still there?" The estate manager replied: "The deal fell through!" Kwek pounced immediately. He contacted the broker right away and thundered: "I can close the deal today." The Singaporean could move even faster than a New Yorker's speed. On the same day, he closed the deal at a mere US$3.4 million.

He bought the air rights to the building and redeveloped it into a 22-storey hotel annex of 130 rooms to Millennium Broadway Times Square. In 1999, the Millennium Premier New York Times Square was opened. A brand new start in old New York. It was a classic Kwek move of shock and awe, revealing an unerring ability to spot good buys at bargain prices.

And if I can make it there
I'll make it practically anywhere
It's up to you
New York, New York
New York

There remained a little piece of treasure which Kwek would savour in between the Millennium Broadway Times Square and the Millennium Premier. The hotel came with one of the oldest surviving

Broadway venues, the Hudson Theatre. The previous owner had converted it into the hotel's event space, but in 2017, Kwek would preside over the reopening of the theatre as a Broadway location. At the time of writing in mid-2022, the Hudson Theatre was showing comedy play *Plaza Suite*, starring New York's entertainment power couple Matthew Broderick and Sarah Jessica Parker. It was like a belated ode to Kwek's most famous purchase in New York after the Millenium and Macklowe — The Plaza Hotel.

As Frank Sinatra sang, if you could make it there in the city of the world, you would make it practically anywhere. More was to come for Kwek in Manhattan.

New York, New York.

Chapter 9

The Plaza

> *"Just who the heck is Kwek?"*
>
> **— Fortune *magazine, December 1995.***

The Plaza Hotel demands attention and gets it. In a city of global icons, from the Statue of Liberty to the Empire State Building, such persistent tenancy of the limelight is worthy of a boast, especially as it has stretched beyond a century, from the 1890s to 2020s. The Plaza, as most New Yorkers called it, knows the world could not afford to ignore its rusticated Vermont marble and cream-coloured terra-cotta brick façade. Perhaps it is because of its fantastic address — preening from a junction of Manhattan which faces Central Park to the north and Fifth Avenue to the west. It carries the ideal blend of sustainability and shopping with the famous urban open space juxtaposing with possibly the world's most luxurious shopping street. The Plaza's zip code is the perfect geography of glamour meets green.

From the day it first opened in 1907, the hotel has always been about glory, glitz and gossip. The first guest through its bronze revolving door was Alfred Gwynne Vanderbilt, one of the United States' wealthiest men. And the "French Renaissance chateau, executed in skyscrapers proportions," in the words of Julie Satow in *The Plaza*, has never stopped welcoming the tycoons and celebrities. American writer F. Scott Fitzgerald famously took a night-time swim in the Pulitzer Fountain outside the marble lobby furnished in the rococo style. He even set a culminating scene in his classic *The Great Gatsby* inside a Plaza room, capturing the glamour and hedonistic times of the pre-Great Depression 1920s.

Such literary representations would continue after the Second World War, with Kay Thompson's *Eloise*, a series of children's books in the 1950s revolving around a main character who lives in the "room on the tippy-top floor" of the hotel. The Plaza's fame would quickly move into films, with Alfred Hitchcock setting his classic *North by Northwest* in the hotel, and later *Home Alone 2* with Macaulay Culkin sharing a scene with a certain Donald Trump at the Plaza's lobby. Of course, the posh building would also have its share of real-life celebrities, from Michael Jackson as a guest to Marilyn Monroe holding a press conference when the spaghetti strap on her dress snapped. Americans even got their first taste of Beatlemania when the British Fab Four stayed in the hotel during their first tour of the US in 1964. The Plaza has long been "a symbol of luxury and grandeur in New York," wrote the *New York Times* in 1995.

When the world's richest nations gathered at the building in 1985 to hammer out a landmark deal named the Plaza Accord to manage the fluctuating value of the US dollar, the hotel was forever written into the history of global finances. From literary to entertainment, from business to geopolitics, the Plaza bewitches and beguiles, charming with its illumination and importance. As one gazes at the thousands of chandeliers from the pristine white architecture, it speaks of awe, said British journalist and travel-writer Stephen Graham. “One stood in the park at nightfall and marvelled. The tiers of irregular light and shade make one think of all humanity living in one building. It is surely one of the most moving sights in New York,” he wrote in *New York Nights* in 1927.

But as the US grappled with a recession in the early 1990s, partly caused by the stock market crash of 1987 and Iraq’s invasion of Kuwait in 1990, the Plaza fell into financial ruin with its owner surrendering the hotel to creditors in 1992. Citibank got the largest pie, but in a depressed market, struggled to find a buyer who would take the New York icon off its hands. For two years, the bank tried and failed.

Then, in 1994, the elite circles of Manhattan began to take note of a serious hotel buyer from a hitherto little-known entity from Singapore called CDL Hotels International Ltd, a subsidiary of City Developments Limited. Not only did CDL buy the Millenium Hotel in downtown, but it also snapped up the Hotel Macklowe in midtown. At its helm was an equally unheard of billionaire named Kwek Leng Beng. A *Fortune* magazine headline in 1995 called the Singaporean “The Mystery Man.”

Such low profile suited Kwek just fine when Citibank approached him to buy the Plaza. While he was immediately intrigued by the prospect, he was as far removed from being seduced by the hotel's glamour and grandiosity as a buyer could be. His response was fairly matter of fact. "One of my principal bankers at Citibank approached me and asked me to look at the Plaza," he told Satow in *The Plaza*. Given the hotel's location and history, he felt that it "had the potential of generating large profits." The banker was Shaukat Aziz, who would later become the Prime Minister of Pakistan. Kwek flew to New York to check out the hotel. "Of course, out of curiosity," he said in an interview for this book.

He liked what he saw. "It's a big animal. It's a beautiful hotel," he said. He was prepared to make a bid when Aziz called him again. This time, the banker was troubled. After a barren two years, Citibank had suddenly found not one, but two buyers. There was another interested buyer who would like to partner Kwek. He was Prince Alwaleed bin Talal of Saudi Arabia, a fellow billionaire who also happened to be Citibank's biggest shareholder. Unlike Kwek, the prince was far better known to the Western elite circles. In 1991, he had stunned the financial world when he bought US$590 million in Citicorp shares, before going on to also own stakes in Euro Disney, Saks Fifth Avenue and Four Seasons Hotel. *The Economist* nicknamed the grandson of King Abdulaziz, the first king of Saudi Arabia, "Warren Albuffett."

Aziz asked Kwek for a "special request" to consider this stranger.

"I don't want to offend my shareholder. Would you consider?" he said, recalled Kwek. The late intervention gave the Singaporean cause for pause. He was about to go in alone. But since there was an option of a partner now, it might not be a bad idea. "I had just bought a lot of hotels, and it would be wise not to overstretch myself," he said. "I remembered my father's words." At the same time, the tie-up with this new face could open up new contacts and opportunities. "From this adventure, I may get to know Prince Alwaleed, and who knows what that can lead to," he said, ever pragmatic.

The prince sent his private jet to pick Kwek up from London, flying him to Riyadh in Saudi Arabia for their first meeting. Alwaleed picked Kwek up himself from the airport. "These princes are very interesting. They always want to drive themselves," he said, still amused after so many years. They drove to a big tent in the middle of the desert at midnight for their first meeting, watched on by Alwaleed's men. "I felt like I was in a movie," said Kwek. "It was really quite an experience." He was impressed with the prince. "He was a good man," he said.

Alwaleed, who was only 40, was impressed with the 54-year-old Singaporean too. He told *Sunday Review*: "I personally admire Mr Kwek's ability to get right to the most important issues in even the most complex transaction, and then to face them head-on." Kwek was flown home in the same jet, with a most unusual present from the Saudi royalty: a gold-dipped AK-47 assault rifle, with its firing pin removed. "I must be the only person in Singapore with an AK-47," he said. The gun still sits proudly in his office.

In April 1995, Kwek and Alwaleed closed the deal to buy the Plaza, stunning an American audience who mostly had no idea who the Singaporean was. *Fortune* wrote: "Chances are, you've heard of Prince Alwaleed bin Talal bin Abdulaziz, a major Citicorp investor who owns a chunk of Saks Fifth Avenue with Investcorp. But just who the heck is Kwek?" What further turned heads was the price which the Singapore-Saudi joint venture paid for this landmark of New York. At US$325 million, Kwek and Alwaleed got an absolute bargain. It was US$83 million less than what the previous owner had paid just seven years earlier in 1988. "When the market hits rock bottom and nobody dares to buy, I come in," Kwek said in an interview with *Reuters* in 1995.

The transaction was a complex one. Essentially, Kwek and Alwaleed agreed to reduce the Plaza's debt from more than US$300 million to about US$25 million. In return, they each received an equity stake of about 42 per cent, with the remainder going to Citibank at 16 per cent. Years later, the pair would buy out Citibank and become 50-50 owners. While previous prospective buyers were scared off by a potentially big renovation bill for the ailing hotel, Kwek and Alwaleed planned to make only minor improvements at US$28 million. Robert I. Small, the president of Fairmont Hotels which was owned by Alwaleed and chosen to manage the Plaza, told the *New York Times*: "Never tamper with greatness. I love it. Why change it?"

The deal made the front page of the *New York Times* when it was announced, firmly catapulting Kwek to international fame. "The Plaza raised our profile overnight," he told Singapore journalists in London a year later, in typical understated fashion. As always, he had impeccable timing. The recession was giving way to an upturn in the mid-1990s and Kwek's prized Manhattan venture was well placed to catch a bull run. As Satow wrote: "Five years into their tenure, the Plaza saw one of its best years ever, with net operating income reaching nearly US$46 million."

It would come to a frightening halt on September 11, 2001, when terrorists crashed two planes into the World Trade Center in Lower Manhattan. Most of the terrorists were from Saudi Arabia, the same country as Alwaleed. The prince's reputation would take a heavy beating when he appeared to justify the attacks by linking it to the Palestinian cause. Although Alwaleed donated US$10 million to assist the victims of 9/11 and their families, New York Mayor Rudy Giuliani rejected it. "Mayor Giuliani told a Saudi prince to take his $10 million donation and stuff it," wrote the *New York Daily News*.

The pressure that was building on the Plaza grew in the following months as tourism to New York dried up in the aftermath of the attacks. After one of its best years, it quickly nosedived by 40 per cent to US$27 million in 2001. By 2003, the Plaza was in the red with a pretax loss of US$1.8 million. To make matters worse, the initial renovation bill of US$28 million had ballooned to US$65 million. Even then, the Grand Old Lady of the Big Apple continued to give problems. "Leaks were a particularly pesky problem. Plastic tarps were tacked up on the ceiling where water dripped into the lobby, and visitors who peeked behind pillars could find buckets discreetly placed to collect additional runoff," wrote Satow. "As many as 30 of the more than 800 rooms were unrentable, suffering from water damage and in need of other repairs."

Kwek did not want to sink more money into the Plaza. He was prepared to sell. Unlike his first love King's Hotel, the Plaza was never an affair of the heart. As he said many times, he does not fall in love easily. After he bought the Plaza in 1995, he told *Fortune*: "We're not short-term investors, but we have to be practical. If somebody in two years offers US$700 million to US$800 million for the Plaza, we say goodbye. Why be sentimental about it? It's an asset."

After September 11, the timing seemed right to let go. There was also a looming shadow over the Plaza which he never quite felt comfortable with and could not shake off. It was that of the man who was forced to sell the hotel to him — a certain Donald Trump.

Chapter 10

When Trump Met Kwek

"I haven't purchased a building. I have purchased a masterpiece — the Mona Lisa."

— Donald Trump on the Plaza in 1988.

Long before Donald Trump descended the golden escalator of his eponymous tower in New York in 2015 to launch an audacious and improbable bid for the United States presidency, he had a far deeper desire that was more posh than political. Since he was seven years old, he had been fascinated by the Plaza Hotel, nursing a desire that would at once lead him to one of his biggest successes, yet also signpost a humiliating defeat. "I just remember the feeling of opulence," he said of his first visit to the hotel. "There's something very haunting and magical about the Plaza."

By 1976, when he was still truly a nobody, he made a bid to own it, offering US$25 million to then owners Westin. When it was rejected, he doubled the offer, according to *Inside the Plaza* by Ward

Morehouse III. It was also turned down, with the top management in Westin saying: "No. And who's Donald Trump?" But Trump, as the world would discover many years later, was not someone easily dissuaded. It was a childhood obsession after all. When he built Trump Tower on Fifth Avenue later on, he made sure he could view the Plaza's copper green mansard roof from his office on the 26th floor. "I was in love with it," he told the *New York Times* in 1988. "I tore myself up to get the Plaza."

For once, he was fairly accurate. Westin was already dying to offload the hotel even before Wall Street crashed in 1987 on Black Monday, accelerating the chain's momentum to sell. Amid dozens of interested buyers, Trump paid over the odds for the Plaza in 1988, handing over US$407.5 million, or US$495,000 per hotel room. It was more than 25 times the hotel's expected earnings. He knew he had made an emotional purchase. "For the first time in my life, I have knowingly made a deal that was not economic," he declared in a full-page advertisement in *New York* magazine showing off his latest trump card. The buy captured the gung-ho capitalism of 1980s New York, said Julie Satow in her book *The Plaza*. "With its prodigious price and Trump's braggadocio, the transaction epitomized the hubris of the go-go '80s, when greed was good and big shoulder pads and even bigger hair was the rage," she wrote.

Trump borrowed the entire sum, plus some more to cover the costs of the transaction and renovations. It was a risky move which would return to bite him badly. But banks were lining up to throw money at him, with Citibank succeeding with the most, offering a total loan of US$425 million. "You cannot believe the money the banks were throwing at us," a former unnamed Trump associate told *Vanity Fair*. "For every deal we did, we would have six or eight banks who were willing to give us hundreds of millions of dollars."

The Plaza became the crown jewel of the Trump empire, a shining palace of haute excess — enormous floral bouquets, deep wine red carpets and gold, gold, plenty of gold. It became the heart of New York tabloid gossip and coverage. "Everyone wanted to come to the Plaza, from Kim Basinger to the Prince of Wales to Mike Tyson," the hotel's manager told Satow.

But trouble mounted soon thereafter as the real estate market in the United States collapsed in the early 1990s. Trump owed his lenders several billion dollars, and would soon lose his yacht, his private jet, his Trump Shuttle airline, stake in Grand Hyatt New York, and most painfully, his Mona Lisa. By 1992, Citibank had effectively taken over the Plaza from Trump. The banks giveth, and the banks taketh away.

The loss was especially painful to Trump, who had once proclaimed the Plaza "the ultimate trophy in the world." He and his lieutenants decided to not go away quietly. Taking defeat badly is a habit which Trump had honed for decades. He believed that if he could find a buyer for the Plaza before Citibank, he might be able to convince the new owner to let him manage the hotel or at least have some role in it. In essence, he wanted a face-saving exit strategy. He found it in Sun Hung Kai, one of the biggest developers in Hong Kong. Trump and his team wooed the Kwoks aggressively and were devastated when they chose not to proceed, after a stay in the Plaza's Presidential Suite ended with a jammed door which had to be hacked apart.

From the Kwoks, Trump quickly turned to the Kweks. When he heard that Citibank had approached Kwek Leng Beng, with Prince Alwaleed bin Talal also interested, Trump focused his firepower on the Singaporean. His right-hand man Abraham Wallach told him to ingratiate himself with Kwek. "I said to Donald, 'I think it would be beneficial for you to meet him and see if a deal could be crafted where you're his partner,'" he told Satow. "You manage the hotel and your position doesn't really change except you got a partner, but nobody ever listens to who the partner is. All they hear is Trump."

Kwek agreed to meet Trump in London. Before the meeting, Citibank banker Shaukat Aziz gave Kwek three tips:

- Trump was a wounded animal. Don't antagonise him further;
- Trump remained very well-connected in New York. Don't make an enemy out of him;
- Trump had a big ego. Let him save face. Pacify him.

Kwek, a master Asian businessman familiar in the art of giving face, knew just what to do. When he arrived at London's Lanesborough Hotel for their breakfast meeting, Trump was already waiting for him at the lobby. He tried to impress the Singaporean immediately. "I just signed an autograph for supermodel Elle Macpherson," said Trump. Kwek was hardly excited. He recalled years later, in the most uninterested deadpan manner: "Heard of her." Trump continued his charm offensive, giving Kwek an autographed copy of his bestselling book *Trump: The Art of the Deal*, and when deciding on breakfast, smiled at Kwek and said: "I'll have whatever you are having!"

Their similarities end with the breakfast choices. While both were, and still are, big players in the global real estate and hospitality, they could not be more different in their approaches to life and work.

- Trump was the champion of excesses, both in substance and style, luxuriating in the high life of private jets and the glitz of celebrities.
- Kwek was low profile and understated, preferring quiet meals, tennis games, and commercial flights.
- Trump loved a good party, especially at the Plaza, where drugs like cocaine were rampant and he was often accompanied by many girls.
- Kwek must be in bed by midnight and once jokingly referred to himself in a media interview as "Cinderella."
- Trump made emotional business decisions, such as the purchase of the Plaza.
- Kwek placed a premium on being consistently rational when weighing up a bid.
- Trump built businesses being leveraged to the hilt, creating

an empire sustained on debts. That's why he lost the Plaza.

- Kwek knew not to overextend credit, carefully choosing partners so as to keep borrowings manageable. That's why he won the Plaza.
- Trump was loquacious.
- Kwek was quiet.

Kwek's first impression of Trump in London? "He talks a lot," he said. The pair did not hit it off. They were too far apart in temperament and style. Trump kept pushing Kwek to make him his partner in the Plaza. But knowing that the American's empire was falling apart and almost broke, Kwek politely declined. Trump changed tack, and asked whether Kwek could let him continue to manage the hotel. Kwek turned him down again, saying that the job was going to Alwaleed's Fairmont Hotels chain. But mindful of Aziz's advice, he gave Trump a face-saving way out. He offered Trump the role of an advisor to the Plaza, with a token fee every year. "It was to pacify him," said Kwek.

In addition, Trump asked to be involved if the Plaza's top floors were converted into penthouses. He told Kwek he knew the New York City authorities and could pave the way for the change. Kwek responded: "Well, it's a good idea." Trump would also get a cut of profits if the condominium penthouses were realised (they weren't), and a small fee if Kwek should sell the hotel within seven years (it wasn't). "I was a good listener when negotiating with Trump," Kwek told Satow. "He wanted to continue managing the hotel and be part of the venture. We eventually narrowed down his role." No drama, no games. Like a kung fu master, he expertly neutralised his opponent's moves without hurting him.

Kwek preferred Alwaleed. "You need two Asian tigers to fight Donald Trump," he said. Boy, did they have a fight on their hands. When Trump failed to convince Kwek to choose him over Alwaleed, he decided to create trouble for the joint venture. When both Kwek's and Alwaleed's executives met in New York to discuss the deal, Trump even planted a spy. When the executives were meeting in the Plaza's Vanderbilt Suite, Wallach was eavesdropping from a secret room, hidden behind a fake wall. "They all come to New York, all the higher-ups on the Saudi side and all the higher-ups on the Kwek side, and where do they decide to stay? In the Plaza Hotel, which is still owned and run by Donald Trump," Wallach said in *The Plaza*. "They're so stupid, they're staying in his property and they don't have a clue."

He made a nuisance of himself, hiding in the cramped space for 10 days. When he heard the Singaporeans and Arabs discussing a US$100 million loan they planned to take out so as to buy the hotel, Wallach also called the same bank and asked for a similar US$100 million loan for the Plaza. He confused the bankers. Trump even pulled the childish stunt of making a fake emergency call, claiming the Plaza was on fire. "You hear FIRE! And then suddenly, all over Fifty-Nine Street and Fifth Avenue, firemen come running into the building with hatchets and hoses, and everybody's required to vacate the building because (it) is deemed structurally unstable," said Wallach. There were days of chaos, when both teams in the new venture were forced to move to another hotel. Trump was proud of his antics. "I drove (Citibank) nuts," he told the *Wall Street Journal*. "I did a number on them that you wouldn't believe."

Citibank caught wind of his mischief and threatened to withhold his other deals if he continued to stymie Kwek and Alwaleed. Trump finally backed down. It was only then that the two Asian tigers succeeded in buying the hotel for US$83 million less than what Trump paid seven years ago. Trump's emotional purchase would turn out to be a very costly error. But Kwek had one last card in his deck. Having witnessed up close the shenanigans of Trump, he wanted to protect the new venture from more of such. So the Singaporean insisted that Citibank remained an equity partner in the deal, ensuring that the bank, which was Trump's main lender, would keep the troublemaker in check.

While Kwek had finally obtained the crown jewel in his burgeoning global hotel empire, he admitted that he was never completely at ease at the Plaza. "Trump's eyes and ears were still in the hotel," he said. "I was always very careful when I stayed in the Plaza." Was he afraid of being bugged? "Who knows?" he replied with a laugh. "He is not someone I want to do business with."

Trump would continue to badger Kwek to give him a bigger role in the Plaza in the next few years, further irritating the Singaporean. "He wanted more than that, but under the circumstances, he couldn't have it," said Kwek in the *Wall Street Journal* in 1997. Decades later, in 2017, when Trump was US President, and Kwek was about to make a visit to New York, he was concerned that the US immigration would intentionally make things difficult for him because of his past rejection of the sitting POTUS.

It was quite different for Alwaleed. He often stayed at the Plaza, and enjoyed holding meetings in its lobby. His Fairmont chain also benefitted from having such a glamorous hotel under its brand. So after September 11, when Kwek was looking to sell the Plaza, Alwaleed demurred. Besides tanking tourism in New York and the Plaza's escalating renovation bill, Kwek said that he wanted rid of the Plaza because of Trump. "He never really let go of The Plaza because of his ego," he said. "This was a man who wanted to dominate everything. And New York was his home ground."

Alwaleed was eventually convinced to let go of the Plaza, and managed to find a buyer who offered US$500 million, a tidy profit from the US$325 million shelled out by him and Kwek. But the Singaporean felt that the hotel was worth far more. He had two options: first, based on the terms of the partnership, he could buy out Alwaleed's stake at the US$500 million valuation and sell it later at a profit since he believed the Plaza was worth more; second, he could find a better buyer with a higher price. He chose the latter. "I could have bought Alwaleed's stake and made a profit later," he shared. "But then Alwaleed would always think that I took advantage of him, that I bought low from him and sold high. He would see me as a dishonest partner and my reputation is worth more than a few hundred millions." Instead, he told the prince to give him some time to get a better price.

The opportunity would present itself a few months later in 2004, when El-Ad Properties, a major Israeli real estate firm, expressed interest in buying the Plaza. Given the sensitivity of Israeli-Arab relations, reaching out to Alwaleed was a no go. El-Ad's broker, Scott Latham, decided to contact Kwek. In an amazing move, he somehow managed to get the private line of Kwek and cold-called the Singaporean. Kwek picked up the phone and surprisingly entertained the stranger on the other line for three minutes, before responding: "Oh, they can't afford it and it's not for sale." Latham asked for a week to prove he had a serious buyer.

Soon, Kwek despatched his loyal lieutenant Wong Hong Ren to New York to meet Latham and El-Ad chief executive Miki Naftali. The Israelis were able to convince Wong that they were indeed credible. They would send a fax to Kwek's office with an offer in June 2004: US$625 million. A week later, Kwek replied through fax that he would finally meet them: July 1, 11am, in Singapore. The Israelis asked for it to be rescheduled, but the Singaporeans gave an ultimatum: be here at that date and time, or forget about it. Naftali and Latham scrambled from Manhattan to reach Singapore early morning on July 1. They made it to Kwek's office in Republic Plaza on July 1, just in time for their 11am meeting.

Kwek met them in his penthouse office, beginning talks which stretched through the day and lunch. Along the way, he fielded calls from other buyers in New York who had gotten word that the Plaza was for sale. "I swear while we were sitting there, Kwek got a phone call and put the receiver down for a minute to tell us that some guy by the name of Lloyd Goldman was on the phone," Latham said in *The Plaza*, referring to one of New York's biggest developers. But Kwek kept talking to his visitors and when the sun was setting, they came to an agreement. El-Ad would pay US$675 million for the Plaza, or US$838,500 per hotel room, a record in New York. It was more than double the US$325 million that Kwek and Alwaleed paid in 1995.

Kwek called Alwaleed and got his approval. By 8pm, both sides inked a one-page memorandum of understanding. "As he had to leave in a hurry, we ended negotiations and shook hands on the deal," Kwek told Satow. Both parties were ecstatic. Kwek called the offer "too good to refuse" in a press conference in Singapore. "The hotel needs renovation and I don't want to spend any more money on it." Although Alwaleed had initial misgivings, he was delighted with the sale too, shared Kwek. "The prince was very happy. He invited me to Paris, where he wanted to give me a big dinner."

The deal put an end to relations between Kwek and Trump, much to the relief of the Singaporean. Kwek said he has never met Trump since, nor kept in contact. When Trump launched his outrageous campaign for the US presidency in 2015, Kwek was surprised. "I did not expect him to win," he said. "And when he won, I was surprised and happy for him. I guess many looked upon him as charismatic."

The trouble of Trump left a sour aftertaste in Kwek. But it did not blemish his nine-year ownership of one of New York's finest icons. Today, he still regarded the Plaza as one of his proudest buys. He said: "It was one of the very iconic purchases, with a very iconic partner, and even more iconic seller!"

CHAPTER 11

The Height of Madness

"That (to sell Copthorne) is the maddest idea...In good times those hotels are a valuable asset..."

— Irish parliamentarian Austin Currie on the Copthorne chain in 1993.

When teenager Anne Klein boarded a flight at Shannon Airport in Ireland, little did she know she would be on a bizarre journey which would eventually end with the Irish national carrier selling one of its biggest assets. The trip had started fairly innocuously in 1995. The 18-year-old checked in for a short flight to Manchester in neighbouring England, but the ground staff of Aer Lingus directed her to a flight to Minsk in Belarus instead. When the cabin crew of the Minsk-bound aircraft discovered they had one too many passengers, they alerted the captain but he chose to continue the flight.

Klein would arrive 1,500 miles later in a strange land with no visa nor a passport, and was promptly locked up. Aer Lingus quickly apologised and arranged accommodation for her in Minsk before flying her to Manchester. "Incidents such as this are extremely rare and very regrettable when they occur," the spokesman of the airline said. "As soon as we realised what had happened we did everything in our power to rectify the situation." But the damage was done. As a commentator noted snarkily: "The attractions of Belarus are no doubt many and the young woman…might have made much of the unexpected chance for sight-seeing which consequently arose. On the other hand, if you are Manchester-bound, Minsk may be a bit exotic."

What made it doubly bad for Aer Lingus was that the embarrassment, which was widely carried in the media, came in the midst of intense financial and regulatory pressure. The airline had been in trouble for some years, brought on by liberalisation in Europe's aviation industry and recession after the Gulf War. The state-owned company had debts of 245 million Irish pounds. Aer Lingus' shareholder, the Irish government, wanted the airline to dispose of its non-core assets and among its most sellable was its Copthorne chain of hotels. The chain was the biggest player in Britain with 12 hotels, including the 833-room Tara in posh Kensington in London, and a few more hotels in Europe. Financial aid from the European Commission also depended on Aer Lingus disposing the hotel chain.

But while Aer Lingus was dying to sell, no one was willing to buy. The depressed property and hotel markets in Europe saw

Copthorne stay on the shelves from 1993 to end 1994, before being removed for sale because no one wanted to pay the asking price of 200 million Irish pounds. The public relations disaster from the Minsk mess further painted Aer Lingus as a desperate seller, with calls for it to pay closer attention to its core business.

Into the midst stepped Kwek Leng Beng, who had moved into the 1990s with an unparalleled hotel expansion business in the world. While negotiating to buy the Plaza in New York in 1994, the Singaporean was told that the Copthorne was available too. "The hotel world knew by then that I was a serious buyer. I don't play the fool," he said. "So as you build a reputation, people will approach you first, before anybody else." He was interested in Copthorne. While he was quite happy to snap up hotels one at a time, such as the Millenium and the Gloucester, this was a chance to grab many in one deal — similar to the coup he pulled off in New Zealand. But unlike the Quality Hotels in a corner of the world, the Copthornes were sitting pretty in the heart of European action. Its nearly 4,000 rooms would boost the stock of hotel rooms under Kwek by 35 per cent to 14,000 rooms. It was the booster shot his burgeoning hotel empire needed.

More than that, he could smell a good bargain. While no one was keen to match Aer Lingus' asking price, he did his research on the Copthorne hotels — including visiting several in person and unannounced — and found that it was good value for money. Most of the hotels sat on freehold land in good locations, with big plots which could easily lend themselves to expansion or other developments. They were also well-built, including superior facilities like swimming pools, gyms and spas — luxurious offerings for a premium four-star hotel experience at that time. "If I were to build, it would take a long time," he said. "Now, with just one deal, I could expand very quickly." The potential of the Copthorne chain was tremendous, and an Irish politician recognised it, calling Aer Lingus' disposal "the height of madness."

If the sellers had taken a temporary leave of sanity, the buyer was clearly in control of his faculties. For two months from July 1995, CDL Hotels and Aer Lingus tussled and thrusted in negotiations in London and Dublin. Kwek led the talks on the Singapore side, and as was his usual style, pressed for swift conclusion with minimal complications. "When you drag out negotiations, you may not get the right price," he said. "My intention is to always move very fast. When they're desperate, you must strike while the iron is hot."

Out went small talk and dinners and drinks. He had little patience to build relations and make friends. Like a true Singaporean, he was every bit as business-like, and some say clinical, as his hometown is known for. "I'm a negotiator who looks at the practical aspects of a deal, whether you like it or not," he shared. "I am very focused on the actual business and I don't like to socialise. I would also secretly go and see some of the hotels. When they question if I have what it takes, I would tell them that if they want to see the colour of my money, they can talk to my banker. My banker would certify that I'm a serious buyer. I've got the money behind me. Let's not waste time."

As negotiations dragged into late July, the Singaporeans pressed for a "lock-out" arrangement that would prevent Aer Lingus from talking to other parties. Other buyers circled, with *The Irish Times* reporting a number of interested US buyers and a British-based group. Among them was Stakis Hotels from Britain. Its then CEO David Michels said: "Leng Beng had access to cash, so his deal was quicker." But by mid-August, both Aer Lingus and CDL Hotels were still struggling to come to an agreement. To make matters worse, a new problem cropped up. Aer Lingus was concerned that a deal could be scuppered by British authorities over antitrust regulations because CDL Hotels would hold a large number of hotels in the country, adding the Copthorne 12 to its existing ones such as the Gloucester, Bailey's and the Knightsbridge in London. The seller wanted its lawyers to research and verify, before putting the call to its board for a decision.

Kwek had had enough. The checks would take weeks and the process could be further delayed by the time Aer Lingus' next board meeting rolled around. He did not want to wait any longer, well aware that a slowdown could jeopardise success. He offered Aer Lingus a way out: he would bear the risks of any British antitrust regulatory roadblocks. In other words, if CDL Hotels were eventually forbidden to buy Copthorne, the burden rested on the Singapore group to dispose of the assets. Aer Lingus was free to collect its money and go on its merry way. In exchange, the airlines would give CDL Hotels a discount on the price. He offered the honey, the other side cut the money. He was, after all, still a shrewd businessman despite his eagerness to close the deal. "Offer a solution that they cannot refuse," he said.

The last hurdle was removed and on August 31, 1995, the deal was sealed and announced. Kwek paid 219 million Irish pounds, or US$337 million, for 16 hotels. It was a game changer. It was the biggest hotel acquisition by a Singapore company in history, and the largest purchase of a British-based hotel group by a Singapore company. It also made CDL Hotels the biggest hotel buyers in the world in the last two years, stunning an industry which had up till then never heard of this Singaporean firm. The Copthorne purchase made CDL Hotels the third biggest hotel owners in the United Kingdom, and swelled Kwek's empire to 53 hotels spanning 11 countries in Asia, Oceania, North America, and Europe. The Singapore company was now among the top 10 international hotel chains in the world.

The Daily Mail in Britain called Kwek the leader of "the world's most acquisitive hotel group." A Singapore-based analyst echoed the comment in an interview with *The Irish Times*. "I would say they are the most aggressive hotel group in the region and even globally, going by their recent purchases," said Leong Chi Meng, investment analyst with Vickers Ballas. Yet, even as the market remained bearish, observers recognised that CDL Hotels had scored a bargain with

Copthorne. The sale price was lower than the book value of the hotels in the Aer Lingus' accounts. In fact, just months after the purchase, he was offered more than 300 million Irish pounds by two hotel chains to part with the Copthorne hotels. *Bloomberg* wrote: "Unlike Japanese hoteliers who bought Western properties at astronomical prices in the late 1980s only to see the market collapse, CDL is trying to build a global empire on the cheap. Its goal is to buy undervalued properties, refurbish them and then wait for the market to turn."

Coming only a month after the Plaza deal, it confirmed in the hotel world that Kwek was a true global hotel mogul with a presence across continents. "Kwek may not have Donald Trump's flamboyant personality, but he is a true risk-taker," said Douglas Hercher, director of Jones Lang Wootton USA in the *New York Times* in 1995. "Anyone who can buy US$1 billion worth of hotels in New York and London in less than two years is in his own way bigger than life."

Even before the Copthorne hotels were in his bag, Kwek was already planning the next move. In April 1995, CDL Hotels formed CDL-USA Management to set the strategy for its growing collection of hotels in New York and London. Just slightly more than a month after Copthorne was snagged, the management revealed plans to consolidate all its hotels in Europe and North America under one name and with a common identity. As a hotel owner and investor, CDL Hotels was largely content with letting outsiders run most of its hotels. But Kwek wanted to build a Singaporean brand that would rival the Hyatts and Sheratons of the world.

Eight months after Copthorne came into CDL Hotels, he listed the Millennium & Copthorne Hotels (M&C) on the London Stock Exchange in April 1996, the first Singapore group to secure a primary listing there. It was done in "turbo-charged speed," as he put it in a media interview. The name drew on his two biggest hotel purchases, the Millenium Hilton in New York and the Copthorne chain in Europe. With it, Kwek rebranded most of his hotels. The luxury five-star establishments like Hotel Macklowe took on the Millennium branding, changing its name to the Millennium Broadway for instance. The tourist-class outfits adopted Copthorne's brand, with the likes of King's Hotel being renamed Copthorne King's Hotel.

The *International Herald Tribune* carried the news with this headline: "A global hotel empire is born." The listing was the first step to a new global strategy where M&C would also expand its hotel empire through management contracts instead of acquiring properties outright. In other words, Kwek's hotel empire would now branch out into using the M&C brands to manage others' hotels and properties, similar to the business strategies of global chains like Marriott and Hilton.

It was quite an unprecedented attempt. While there were astounding regional successes from Asia, such as Malaysian Robert Kuok's Shangri-La, Indonesian Adrian Zecha's Aman Resorts and Singaporean Ho Kwon Ping's Banyan Tree, no Asian chains had taken the fight to the major US and European brands on their own turfs.

But then again, Kwek loved nothing more than being a trend-setter. On the eve of M&C's listing, he told the media: "My advantage (over other hoteliers) is that I am not only a hotel person, but also a real-estate person and a financial person." From Hong Kong to Hollywood, from Manchester to Minsk. The world had been served notice.

Part 4

Top Gun

”

Today, our flagship building stands as a testimony to our long-term business strategy and the successful handover of CDL's first-generation leaders to the second generation.

— Kwek Leng Beng

CHAPTER 12

Standing Tallest

"A symbol of private sector determination and courage to forge ahead despite the odds."

— then Singapore Prime Minister Goh Chok Tong when opening the Republic Plaza in 1998.

Ask Kwek Leng Beng about any financial crises, economic recessions and global meltdowns, and his reactions are almost always a dull stare into space at a seemingly boring question, followed by a gentle shrug. "We are conservative, we don't borrow a lot," he said. "I would tell my staff, have no fear. It doesn't bother me." For a man who has adroitly followed his father's contrarian business acumen of seizing opportunities in crises, a bearish market is when he transforms into a bull. Through oil crises, recessions, race riots and even the sudden independence of his country, nothing had fazed Kwek and Hong Leong.

The Asian Financial Crisis of 1997 was the exception. On July 2, the Thai government buckled and could not maintain the strength of its currency against the dollar. The collapse of the baht was followed by a swift contagion across the region, ailing South Korea,

Indonesia and others. As governments fell and billionaires turned bankrupt overnight, even Kwek admitted that the jitters got to him for the first time since he took over leadership of Hong Leong in 1990. "I've seen many crises. But, you know, at that time, it was quite frightening," he said.

In October 1997, he found himself S$200 million poorer in just one day. His stake in City Developments Limited (CDL) and Hong Leong Finance dropped from S$2.95 billion to S$2.73 billion overnight. CDL shares which were trading at S$14.50 apiece at the start of the crisis nosedived 55 per cent to S$6.45. "Everything seemed to be collapsing. Everybody was so frightened," he recalled.

Yet, while he suffered eye-popping losses on paper, his business was largely unscathed by the deep chilly winds which blew across Asia in 1997. Thanks partly to his acquisitions of hotels in the United States and Europe in the years leading up to the crisis, and his companies' low gearing, he avoided the bloodbath that engulfed his own Asian backyard, reported *The Straits Times* in 1998. "So it is no surprise that his stable of companies, which includes Hong Leong Holdings and City Developments, has not been singed by the regional currency firestorm."

Instead, he would revel in the completion of the largest, and possibly most complicated, project in Hong Leong's history — a dream to build and own the tallest building in Singapore. When the Republic Plaza was ready in 1998, it could not be a more incongruent scene. Six months into the Asian Financial Crisis, in January 1998, he opened his company's new flagship headquarters in the heart of Singapore's financial district. It was mainly about the optics. The building was completed before the crisis engulfed Asia. But at a time when half-completed buildings were left abandoned across Southeast Asia, offering hulks of cement carcasses as reminders of the meltdown, CDL officially unveiled its single largest investment ever — a S$650 million skyscraper. It was a jarring image that probably filled the contrarian Kwek with more than his usual delight. When then Singapore Prime Minister Goh Chok Tong opened Republic Plaza, he praised it as "a symbol of private sector determination and courage to forge ahead despite the odds."

It was also a symbol of business foresight, long-term planning and inter-generational succession. Amazingly, CDL did not have to pay to build their rocket-shaped flagship, which rivalled the defunct OUB Centre and UOB Plaza as the joint-tallest skyscrapers in Singapore at that time. All they did was to contribute two plots of land, shared an unnamed senior CDL official to the media in 1988. "The beautiful thing about this huge project is that we won't see people running about trying to raise money," he said. "We're not going to cough out a single cent for this project."

The ingenuity was started by Kwek Hong Png, and completed by Kwek Leng Beng. In 1987, Kwek senior bought two plots of land in Singapore's central business district from the Oversea-Chinese Banking Corporation (OCBC) at S$51.3 million, or S$3,000 per square foot. To convince OCBC to sell, he personally visited OCBC's honorary life president Tan Chin Tuan, said CDL's group general manager Chia Ngiang Hong, who accompanied Kwek senior to the meeting. "The face is very important for all these old legendary business people," he recalled. "When our old chairman appeared, the other side had to reciprocate and give him face. Their negotiations were cordial and everything was conducted in Hokkien."

The purchases heralded Hong Leong's first entry into Raffles Place, the most-sought-after prime address in the financial downtown. The price was not cheap. CDL paid three times more for its land parcels than the adjacent real estate, an unusual phenomenon for a company known for entering during depressed markets rather than buying on a high. But the aberration was necessary. Kwek senior was not interested in the two plots in and of themselves. What he was eyeing was "the chance to take part in the biggest office project to be launched in Singapore," reported *The Business Times*.

The reason is because his new purchases were right smack in the middle of a new mega commercial project to be built, one which had already been named Republic Plaza. The project was led by a consortium made up of Japanese firm C Itoh and Australia's Land Equity. The group had already bought five parcels of land to build Republic Plaza, until they invited Kwek to combine their land with his two plots into an even larger building. "Together they will hold almost 9,300 sq m of prime land adjacent to the Raffles Place Mass Rapid Transit (MRT) station," said *The Business Times*, which added that the project would likely be one of the last projects in Raffles Place for some time.

Amid mounting speculation that Land Equity lacked the resources to continue with the project, and was looking to sell parts of the project to foreign banks, the consortium merged with CDL. After eight months of what Kwek Leng Beng described as "quiet negotiations" headed personally by his father, CDL went from outsider in the Republic Plaza project to being the biggest shareholder. In April 1988, it was announced that CDL would own 50 per cent stake in the joint-venture company to build Republic Plaza, with C Itoh, Land Equity and Japanese construction firm Shimizu holding the remaining shares.

That is not all. When the building was completed, CDL would buy out the joint-venture partners at cost plus a fixed percentage of profit. C Itoh was the only one who retained an option to hold on to 11.25 per cent interest. In addition, C Itoh would provide CDL with an eight-year loan to fund the purchases. In 1990, amid delays in the project, Land Equity pulled out of the joint venture, selling its 20 per cent stake to CDL for S$19.5 million in cash. In exchange, CDL increased its holding of Republic Plaza to 70 per cent.

Kwek Hong Png would not live to see the completion of Republic Plaza, but his successor would finish the job beautifully. After he died in 1994, Kwek Leng Beng took over and when the main building was finally completed in 1996, CDL bought out the Japanese partners' remaining 30 per cent stake based on the 1988 agreement at a pre-fixed formula. It paid S$47 million, or in the words of a commentator: "It may not be the deal of a century, but (it) surely comes close to it." The purchase valued each square foot of lettable space in freehold Republic Plaza at S$1,200, at a time when nearby leasehold land was sold at S$2,200. *The Business Times* called CDL's buy a "great deal," adding: "By today's standards, this is an absurdly low price."

Kwek ensured that despite a generational and leadership change in Hong Leong, there was barely a kink in the decade-long development plan of Republic Plaza. "In the late 1980s, the site on which Republic Plaza stands today consisted of separate titles by different owners, and numerous attempts by various developers to combine them into one larger unit failed," he said at the opening in 1998. "Displaying his usual flair and sound business judgment, my father negotiated quietly and successfully to acquire the vital plot of land."

The 66-storey building may not have achieved his father's dream of one with 88 floors, but it still managed to be joint-tallest in Singapore at 280m, until it was overtaken by Guoco Tower (283.7m) in 2016 and the Skywater Residences (formerly known as the AXA Tower) (305m) to be completed in 2026. "Against the odds at that time, when the economy was facing a slump in the 1980s, CDL held on to its bold vision of establishing a world-class landmark on the Singapore skyline," continued Kwek. "Today, our flagship building stands as a testimony to our long-term business strategy and the successful handover of CDL's first-generation leaders to the second generation."

The Asian Financial Crisis barely had a dent on its birth. Right before the recession hit in 1997, CDL signed 90 per cent of the tenants in Republic Plaza to six-year leases that would run till 2002. The company would bank S$80 million in annual rental income in 1998 from Republic Plaza alone, making a mockery of the weak market and record office vacancies in Singapore then. Indeed, when CDL announced its 1998 numbers in the first quarter of 1999, its results were at odds with its competitors. Eight out of 10 listed real estate companies sank into the red amid a sharp plunge in property prices. CDL was one of only two to still stay in the black. It scored S$123.7 million in profits, although that was a 70 per cent drop. "The performance, achieved against the backdrop of the worst year in the Asian meltdown and the sharp downturn in property prices, is, in the opinion of the board, very satisfactory," the company said in a statement.

The Business Times said that given the bloodbath which had slaughtered property counters, "few could quarrel with that." CDL was the only property company that saw its shareholders' funds expand in 1998, from S$3 billion to S$3.13 billion. In fact, the paper went so far as to praise CDL as a favourite of foreign fund managers, and considered by them as "the only property blue chip in Singapore."

While the Asian Financial Crisis did enough to spook Kwek for once, the nerves hardly translated into genuine fears. As he said at the opening of Republic Plaza: "In all sectors of business, CDL's guiding principle has always been to look for opportunities in depressed market conditions. In the face of adversity, there are always opportunities." As he rode towards the new millennium, he would live up to that dictum once again. When others got on their knees, he would stand tallest. Crisis be damned.

Kwek Hong Png came to Singapore as a penniless migrant and built Hong Leong from scratch in 1941.

A rare photo of young Kwek Leng Beng (standing, right), with (from left) sister Kwek Geok Luan, mother Tan Cheng Neo, cousin Quek Leng Chan, and their grandmother Yap Kan Neo.

The family bungalow at Buckley Road bought in 1943 during the Japanese Occupation. Kwek moved in at five, along with his uncles, aunties and cousins.

Kwek (left) and Leng Chan (right) in their childhood (top) and teenage days (bottom). Leng Chan is the head of the Hong Leong group in Malaysia.

A wedding photo of Kwek and Cecilia, who got married in 1970. Cecilia recalled spending many nights in the early years of their marriage at the lobby of King's Hotel and Orchid Inn (now an upscale condominium development, The Glyndebourne), where Kwek would pace around to gauge how many guests were checking in.

Kwek with Cecilia, whom he first met when she was working as a lawyer in Singapore, on their honeymoon in London.

Kwek and Cecilia with their sons, Kingston (left) and Sherman (right).

Pictured (from left): Kwek, Sherman, Kwek's stepmother Wee Siew Cheng, Kingston, patriarch Kwek Hong Png, and Cecilia.

Kwek (centre in suit) and his team at the opening of the Hong Leong Finance (HLF) Lavender Street branch in 1967. Today, HLF has become the largest finance company in Singapore with 28 branches and 12 SME Centres across the island.

Pictured (from left): Kwek Leng Joo, Kwek Geok Luan, Quek Bee Heong (carrying Jeanette Hangchi), Vincent Yeo, Wee Siew Cheng, Kevin Hangchi, Kwek Hong Png, Sherman, Kwek Lee Hoon, Cecilia, Kwek, Gan Khai Choon, Patricia Yeo, David Yeo, and Kenneth Hangchi. This photo was taken during Kwek Hong Png's birthday celebration in late 1979 at his home.

Kwek posing in front of his favourite cars from luxury brand Aston Martin, including the DB7 (below). He had a well-known fondness for cars and would frequently visit dealerships to learn more about the car business, especially after focusing a large part of HLF's business on motor vehicle loans.

Top: The late Hong Leong founder aided by his two sons, Leng Joo (left) and Kwek (right), used property developer City Developments Limited (CDL) to grow the family business.

Leng Joo's untimely death in 2015 dealt a major blow to his brother and the family business. He is remembered for kickstarting CDL's sustainability efforts as its managing director in 1995, a time when corporate social responsibility had not yet taken hold, and was often the face of its philanthropic work.

Left: One year after Hong Leong took control of the management of CDL in 1973, Kwek was appointed managing director. CDL rode the wave of development in Singapore and transformed into the property giant it is today. At its former headquarters at City House (seen here), Kwek was famously known for "scolding" the lift for being too slow.

King's Hotel was Hong Leong's first venture into Singapore's booming tourism sector and hotel industry. It was positioned as a hotel for middle-income tourists and remains Kwek's "first love." King's Hotel officially opened in 1970 and is known as Copthorne King's Hotel today.

Kwek receiving the 1996 Businessman of the Year Award by *The Business Times*, a harbinger of the conglomerate that Hong Leong would go on to build in the sectors of real estate, finance and hotels.

Kwek receiving a special edition of *The Singapore Story: Memoirs of Lee Kuan Yew* at then Senior Minister Lee Kuan Yew's 75th joint birthday celebration and book launch.

In April 1995, Kwek, together with Prince Alwaleed bin Talal of Saudi Arabia, bought the Plaza from Donald Trump, many years before the New York tycoon would run for presidency in the United States. Till this day, it is known as Kwek's most famous purchase.

Impressed by Kwek, Prince Alwaleed gifted him a most unusual present: a gold-dipped AK-47 assault rifle, with its firing pin removed. The gun still sits proudly in Kwek's office today.

Leng Beng, Prince Alwaleed say yes to US$675m deal they can't refuse

Duo rake in fat profit from sale of their famous New York Plaza hotel

By **Kalpana Rashiwala**

[SINGAPORE] For hotel and property magnate Kwek Leng Beng and billionaire Saudi investor Prince Alwaleed, there are offers so enticing that even they could not walk away from.

Indeed, the duo have just sold their famed Plaza hotel in New York for US$675 million in a deal that Mr Kwek described yesterday as simply "too good for us to refuse".

The deal will net a handsome profit for the two men, who bought the hotel in 1995 in a high-profile deal that valued the asset at US$325 million.

The hotel is owned equally by Mr Kwek's London listed Millennium & Copthorne Hotels (M&C) and his Saudi partner.

Mr Kwek said the US$675 million sale price exceeded his maximum price expectation of US$500 to US$550 million, or 10 times potentially improved earnings before interest and tax (ebit) of US$50 to US$55 million a year from the historic hotel.

Even in the best of times, in 2000, the hotel used to generate ebit of US$45 million. By changing the guest mix and making other improvements, it may be possible to boost annual ebit to US$50 to US$55 million, Mr Kwek said.

"So we felt this is the right opportunity, right timing," he added.

"He (Prince Alwaleed) is very happy. He has invited me to Paris. He wants to give me a big dinner," said Mr Kwek.

"I am very happy (to announce the sale), although in some ways I'm nostalgic about it. This is an icon and it's facing Central Park," he said of the hotel on Fifth Avenue.

The acquisition in 1995 of the New York landmark frequented by the wealthy and powerful shot Mr Kwek to international fame. His partner in the purchase sent his jet to London to fly Mr Kwek to his palace in Riyadh. Mr Kwek was wooed and he agreed to let the Prince's Fairmont hotel chain manage The Plaza.

The Prince's parting gift for Mr Kwek before he flew back home? A golden machine gun.

Mr Kwek said yesterday of the sale: "Why do I want to be emotional about it? The hotel needs renovation and I don't want to spend money anymore. I want to maximise shareholder value." The 1995 purchase valued the hotel and an adjoining property at US$325 million. A further US$35 million to US$40 million was spent sprucing up the hotel. M&C and Prince Alwaleed have "already taken out some money from the asset", Mr Kwek said yesterday.

The hotel was revalued at the end of last year and some of this went into M&C's books. Analysts suggested that assuming M&C is carrying the hotel at US$425 million in its books, gross profit from the sale before factoring in transaction costs would be about US$250 million.

M&C's half share of this would work out to US$125 million.

More importantly, the sale will release cashflow of about US$430 million, after factoring in outstanding loans on the asset of US$245 million. M&C's half-share of this cashflow would be US$215 million.

The sale, to an affiliate of US property investment company El Ad Properties NY LLC, is slated for completion by year's end. If everything goes according to plan, M&C and its Singapore-listed parent, City Developments, should be able to book their respective shares of gains from the sale in Q4.

Despite the sale of the Plaza, Mr Kwek stressed that "the group's strategy of being an owner of hotels assets remains unchanged, especially in an improving trading environment".

And he's not following the current fashion of many hotel groups of going asset light by selling their hotels and relying on getting management contracts as such contracts do not generate as much income as operating your own hotels, said Mr Kwek.

More importantly, from a real estate viewpoint, "in a rising market when the market is recovering — just as we are now in that phase — you make a lot more money by retaining your asset rather than selling it out and then taking a management contract on it," said Mr Kwek.

"Many analysts and institutions in London have been asking me: 'Why don't you follow the new trend?' If I had listened to them, today I would not be making money out of The Plaza. They have been bugging me from Day One. When I floated M&C, they said: 'Why don't you sell The Plaza? I said: 'Why should I sell? I know The Plaza is going to make me good money.' "

"At that time, when they were suggesting we sell, it was probably about US$400 million. In the best of years, 2000, Plaza was probably worth US$500 million.

"Today we are able to sell because the buyer offered us a price that factors in the potential. There is one and only one Plaza in the world.

Citing another example of how M&C could potentially extract more value out of its real estate, Mr Kwek said that two of its UK hotels, Copthorne Tara in Kensington and Copthorne Effingham Park at Gatwick, had enough room to house "mega casinos" of about 50,000 sq ft after the liberalisation of gaming laws in UK that are expected to kick in towards the end of the year.

This will attract American casino operators and owners who'll want to operate a different model from the standard London casino.

Ahead of these changes, potential buyers for these hotels have been knocking on M&C's door. "But because I know the gaming law is changing, why do I want to sell at this time?" said Mr Kwek.

"But if somebody wants to buy the hotels at a ridiculous price and again make an offer that I cannot refuse, I will consider it seriously."

CHRIS LOH

Two men and a hotel: *Clockwise from left — Mr Kwek, Prince Alwaleed bin Talal, and the Plaza hotel. Mr Kwek said that despite the sale of the Plaza, M&C's strategy of being an owner of hotel assets remains unchanged.*

CityDev posts *$37m Q2 profit, Pg 4*

Nine years after buying the Plaza, one of New York's finest icons, Kwek sells the hotel to El-Ad Properties, a major Israeli real estate firm.

Unlike King's Hotel, Kwek was prepared to sell the Plaza when the time was ripe. Nevertheless, he regards it as one of his proudest buys as a businessman.

Kwek listed the Millennium & Copthorne Hotels (M&C) on the London Stock Exchange in April 1996, becoming the first Singapore group to secure a primary listing there. The M&C name laid the basis for the rebranding of most of the hotels in his empire.

Kwek and Sherman spending time together in the United Kingdom.

Kwek meeting former British Prime Ministers Margaret Thatcher (above) and John Major (top right), as well as Boris Johnson, then Mayor of London (right). Kwek made frequent trips to London after CDL's Copthorne purchase of 16 hotels in 1995 made it the third biggest hotel owner in the UK. In March 2023, CDL also acquired the historic waterfront landmark St Katharine Docks, increasing the group's total commercial assets in Britain to £1 billion.

Five-star deluxe hotel The Biltmore Mayfair, previously known as the Millennium Hotel London Mayfair before its reopening.

In January 1998, Hong Leong's new flagship headquarters Republic Plaza opened in the heart of Singapore's financial district, sharing the joint title of Singapore's tallest building with One Raffles Place and UOB Plaza at the time. When then Singapore Prime Minister Goh Chok Tong opened Republic Plaza, he praised it as "a symbol of private sector determination and courage to forge ahead despite the odds."

The Sail @ Marina Bay is the first major condominium in the central business district and then tallest residential building in Singapore at 245m high, offering an expansive view of the sea. CDL launched its first tower in 2004 and the second a year later, after the government announced the building of an integrated resort at the Marina Bay.

The Hudson Theatre, one of New York's oldest surviving Broadway venues, reopened in February 2017, with actor Jake Gyllenhaal making his Broadway musical debut. It sits between the Millennium Premier New York Times Square which opened in 1999, and the Millennium Hotel Broadway Times Square that Kwek first bought in 1994.

Pictured (from left): Julie Menin (member of the New York City Council from District 5), Annaleigh Ashford (actress), Jake Gyllenhaal, Kwek, and Eric Paris (General Manager at the Hudson Theatre) [Photo courtesy of Ambassador Theatre Group.]

Kwek made his New York breakthrough with the sleek Millenium Hotel in downtown Manhattan, which was rebranded as Millennium Downtown New York Hotel in 2022. After the September 11 attacks, the hotel, right across the street from the World Trade Center, suffered severe damage. CDL would spend the next 18 months rebuilding it.
[Photo courtesy of L.E. Baskow / Left Eye Images.]

After a US$32-million makeover, the Millenium reopened in March 2003 to much fanfare, with Cecilia (middle), then New York Governor George Pataki (red tie) and then New York City Mayor Michael Bloomberg (blue tie) at its official launch.

Kwek at The St. Regis Singapore's ground-breaking ceremony in 2004 (top) and at its official opening with Cecilia in April 2008 (left). It is widely considered as one of Singapore's best hotels.

Kwek at the unveiling of the Marina Bay Sands project with architect Moshe Safdie (top, right) and Las Vegas Sands boss Sheldon Adelson (bottom, left).

[Sources: (top) *The Business Times* © SPH Media Limited. Permission required for reproduction. (bottom) *The Straits Times* © SPH Media Limited. Permission required for reproduction.]

Kwek at the W Singapore – Sentosa Cove grand premiere opening party in 2012. The five-star luxury hotel is located in Sentosa Cove, just minutes away from downtown Singapore.

Pictured (from left): Stephane Fabregoul (General Manager of W Singapore – Sentosa Cove), Leng Joo (Managing Director of CDL), Lim Hng Kiang (then Minister for Trade and Industry), Kwek, and Stephen Ho (President of Starwood Hotels & Resorts Asia Pacific)

Kwek giving a speech at the grand premiere, where he said that the opening of W Singapore – Sentosa Cove, together with Quayside Isle, would add to the vibrancy of Sentosa Cove by providing a marina lifestyle haven unlike anything ever before.

Kwek at the unveiling of the Marina Bay Sands project with architect Moshe Safdie (top, right) and Las Vegas Sands boss Sheldon Adelson (bottom, left).

[Sources: (top) *The Business Times* © SPH Media Limited. Permission required for reproduction. (bottom) *The Straits Times* © SPH Media Limited. Permission required for reproduction.]

Kwek at the W Singapore – Sentosa Cove grand premiere opening party in 2012. The five-star luxury hotel is located in Sentosa Cove, just minutes away from downtown Singapore.

Pictured (from left): Stephane Fabregoul (General Manager of W Singapore – Sentosa Cove), Leng Joo (Managing Director of CDL), Lim Hng Kiang (then Minister for Trade and Industry), Kwek, and Stephen Ho (President of Starwood Hotels & Resorts Asia Pacific)

Kwek giving a speech at the grand premiere, where he said that the opening of W Singapore – Sentosa Cove, together with Quayside Isle, would add to the vibrancy of Sentosa Cove by providing a marina lifestyle haven unlike anything ever before.

Upscale waterfront shopping centre Quayside Isle is located next to W Singapore – Sentosa Cove and is the first and only dining and retail destination within the integrated luxury waterfront enclave.

Kwek, his aunt Tan Poh Hua (left) and Cecilia at his cousin Leng Chan's 70th birthday celebration in Las Vegas. After his mother's death, his aunt, Leng Chan's mother, was his key caregiver.

Kwek and Cecilia with Lawrence Wong, then Acting Minister for Culture, Community and Youth and Senior Minister of State for Communications and Information, at the 2012 groundbreaking ceremony for the expansion of the Kwek Hong Png Gallery at the Asian Civilisations Museum.

Nearly seven decades after his father started Hong Leong as a general trading company with a shopfront by the southern shores of Singapore, Kwek would complete the development of The South Beach on the exact same road in 2016. The commercial and residential complex was a fine addition to Kwek's properties across the new waterfront of his hometown, from The Sail through Sentosa to Beach Road.

CDL celebrated its 50th anniversary with a Golden Gala dinner in 2013 at W Singapore – Sentosa Cove. The event was graced by then Deputy Prime Minister Teo Chee Hean, seen here at the anniversary cake cutting with Kwek and his brother Leng Joo (third from right).

Kwek and Cecilia at CDL's 50th anniversary Golden Gala. In his anniversary message, Kwek attributed CDL's success to his late father, whom he felt laid the foundations for the company to thrive both locally and internationally.

Kwek with internationally-acclaimed French designer Philippe Starck at the grand opening of his M Social chain of hotels in Singapore in May 2016.

Kwek adding a new Lifetime Achievement Award to his collection at the Asia Pacific Entrepreneurship Awards in 2017. The award recognises his outstanding entrepreneurship in leading Hong Leong for the last five decades.

Pictured (from left): Kingston, Cecilia, Kwek, and Sherman

In 2015, Kwek became the first Singaporean to receive the Lifetime Achievement Award from the Hotel Investment Conference Asia Pacific (HICAP), which honours exceptional individuals who have advanced the hotel industry in the Asia-Pacific region and the world.

Kwek receiving the SG50 Outstanding Chinese Pioneers Award from then President Tony Tan in 2015, which recognises outstanding Chinese business pioneers and their contributions towards nation-building.

Kwek meeting former US President George W. Bush (top) and founder of Microsoft Bill Gates (bottom).

Then Minister for Education Heng Swee Keat (middle) presenting the inaugural Real Estate Developers' Association of Singapore (REDAS) Lifetime Achievement Award to Kwek in 2014. The award recognises the loyal patron's consistent and significant contributions to the community and the built environment. They are accompanied by then REDAS President Chia Boon Kuah (right).

Kwek Leng Joo (left) sharing with Kwek about an artwork showcased at "Timeless Jiangnan", the first exhibition by the late Kwek Leng Joo. It was jointly organised by him and award-winning Singaporean watercolourist Mr Ong Kim Seng in 2002.

Bought by Kwek in November 1999, the five-star Millennium Hilton Seoul was a staple in Itaewon's skyline, the heart of the Korean capital's commercial and entertainment area. Its sale in 2021 would reverse two years of gloomy fortunes for CDL and the Kwek family, with the highest net profit achieved by CDL since its founding in 1963.

Kwek at his 81st birthday celebration, where he had expressed his love for working and joked that he "still has a good decade to go."

Kwek visiting The Bailey's Hotel in Kensington, London during Christmas in 2022. It is his favourite hotel in England, according to former Hilton CEO Sir David Michels (bottom right).

Kwek with his long-time friend and London flatmate, Yeoh Cheng Kung, having breakfast at Tiong Bahru Market after a morning walk. Yeoh was also a lifelong Hong Leong employee, having served as the former King's Hotel general manager.

Kwek on his morning walk along the Singapore River, with the Grand Copthorne Waterfront standing tall in the background.

Kwek and his extended family at his joint birthday celebration with his elder sister Geok Luan (seated on his left) on January 27, 2023.

Kwek and Cecilia celebrating their wedding anniversary with their two sons and their wives.

Kwek and his immediate family, including his four grandchildren.

Kwek stuck to his father's succession playbook, keeping it within the family and bringing Sherman (left) into the business early on to create a long runway for a smooth handover. Also, his nephew Eik Sheng (right) is chief operating officer of CDL.

Shanghai Mayor Gong Zheng (fourth from right) receiving Kwek, Sherman and the CDL delegation in 2023 at a meeting to discuss sustainable projects in the city.

In August 2023, Kwek and CDL jointly donated S$24 million to the Singapore Institute of Technology (SIT) to establish the Kwek Leng Beng University Tower under his name in its new campus in Punggol. This was in addition to his contribution earlier in the year, which allowed for the start of six new academic initiatives, including bursaries and scholarships, for SIT Hospitality Business undergraduates.

CDL celebrating its 60th anniversary with a Diamond Jubilee Celebration at Orchard Hotel Singapore in 2023, which was graced by Guest-of-Honour Deputy Prime Minister and Minister for Finance Lawrence Wong. The framed calligraphy piece (seen below) was gifted to CDL by an esteemed guest and roughly translates to "three generations of painstaking effort, 60 years of honour and glory."

The Singapore EDITION Hotel opened in late 2023 in the premier Orchard Road belt in Kwek's hometown, adding yet another luxurious gem to his hotel empire. The hotel is integrated with ultra high-end residential development Boulevard 88.

The author Peh Shing Huei (second from right) and his colleagues interviewing Kwek in his office at Republic Plaza for *Strictly Business*.

CHAPTER 13

Millennium Mogul

"What Kwek Leng Beng has achieved in the last 10 years is monumental."

— Adrian Zecha, founder of Regent and Aman hotel chains, in 2000.

When Asia sneezes, Kwek Leng Beng seizes. While the region was bedridden by the Asian economic flu in 1998, the Singaporean consolidated his defences and made sure the financial health of his companies would hold steady. Once his backline was secured, he went on the offensive as the decade turned into its last year. The world may have been slowed by the Millennium Bug, but Kwek would hasten to add booster shots that would take him into the 2000s with fresh landmarks, milestone victories and global accolades. As he approached his 60th birthday, he was morphing into a millennium mogul at the top of his game.

In January 1999, word hit the markets that Kwek was embarking on his biggest and most audacious hotel acquisition which could top US$1 billion. As Hong Kong's Century Group languished since the onset of the regional financial crisis, it had been desperately trying to reduce its massive debt burden. The company had bought properties in Hong Kong and hotels in the United States at very high prices, including US$100 million for the 326-room Meridien in Boston. This put its Regal chain of hotels in heavy debt, owing banks HK$9 billion, or about S$1.9 billion then. But the chain with some 50 hotels was also Century's most sellable asset. If they could dispose the hotels in one block, it would alleviate the financial woes of the Lo family behind Century, led by Lo Ka Shui.

The Regal hotels fit neatly into Kwek's global strategy. He had built up a significant portfolio of hotels across Asia and Australasia before the Copthorne bite gave him strong presence in Europe. But the US was still missing. He had three hotels in New York, including the Plaza, but nothing farther west. The Regal would, in his own words, be the "last piece of the jigsaw puzzle" to complete a worldwide hotel network.

The chain had luxury properties in US gateway cities like New York, Chicago and Los Angeles, such as the United Nations Plaza, the Biltmore and the Knickerbocker respectively. Regal was also found in Boston, Minneapolis, St Louis, Cincinnati, Boulder, Nashville and Anchorage. Its capture would give Kwek a massive presence in the US, the world's largest hotel market, from the east to the west coast. As the Americans would say, from sea to shining sea. The Singaporean's hotels were stretching across the Anglo-Saxon world, from New Zealand in the south to the Great Britain and across the Atlantic in the US. If the sun never set on the British empire in the 19th century, the same hyperbole could be applied to Kwek's new global hotel empire.

Unlike many of his counterparts in Asia, he had the financial muscle to swallow the chain. After the listing of Millennium & Copthorne (M&C) in London in 1996, he moved to restructure the company by selling all of his other hotels in Asia and Australasia to M&C. The change gave M&C a formidable war chest to draw up a hit list of hotels to buy. "We have £206 million in cash and £700 million in rights shares from the restructuring," said a CDL spokesman in May 1999. "We are cash-rich and ready to look for opportunities anywhere around the world." Regal was the top choice.

While Western buyers circled over Regal, Kwek used his personal friendship with Lo to edge ahead. He said in 1999: "A lot of Americans wanted to buy the Regal chain. They talked to Lo, thinking that they could buy the chain at a bargain because he was desperate to sell. If you talk to Asians like that, they will say: 'Go to hell'." Instead, Kwek engaged Lo as an equal and showed him respect and deference. He was only too acutely aware of the upheavals of business. A wounded entrepreneur today could quickly turn around tomorrow; no one was immune. "I praised him on how he managed to have the Regal chain, and told him that regardless of what happened, I would always hold him in high regard," said Kwek.

In November 1999, Kwek concluded what the media called a "whopper deal," worth US$640 million. It bought him 47 Regal hotels in US, of which 28 are owned and the remaining 19 are management contracts. All of them were to be renamed under the Millennium brand, which joined the league of the world's 15 biggest hotel operators, with 33,000 hotel rooms in 117 hotels across 13 countries.

The Regal buy was the second largest ever by a Singapore company, behind Neptune Orient Line's US$825-million purchase of US-based shipping line APL. "The Regal purchase enables the group to acquire in a single stroke a number of landmark hotels in some of the key cities in USA, which is the world's largest hotel market," said Kwek in the news announcement. "We believe that the price we paid is in line with the current conditions. It is a fair price. And more importantly, the landmark hotels are of strategic importance to us, in view of our intention to become a truly global hotel operator."

A week before the Regal was sealed, Kwek would stun the world with a lightning quick purchase of the Seoul Hilton, one of the best hotels in South Korea. And just like Regal, it was also a distressed sale amid the rolling fallout from the Asian Financial Crisis. The hotel was the prized asset of South Korea's Daewoo Group, whose debts amounted to a quite unbelievable US$66 billion. The conglomerate was trying to sell its assets as part of a government-ordered restructuring plan for the nation's top five *chaebols*, aimed to improve efficiency and boost foreign investors' confidence.

Daewoo put the Seoul Hilton on the market reluctantly. The 673-room hotel in Itaewon, the heart of the Korean capital's commercial and entertainment area, was the group's pride. "Daewoo used only the best materials for this hotel, filled with artwork and sculptures curated by the boss' wife. It was like her own palace," said Kwek. "It was a very well-built hotel that was enjoying very strong occupancy." The 22-storey on freehold land — his favourite — also boasted Korea's largest convention hall at more than 25,000 sq ft. Everything about Seoul Hilton spoke to his business heart and mind.

But Daewoo had already found a buyer, the Luxembourg-based investment company General Mediterranean Holding. Talks were going on smoothly for some months, before they surprisingly collapsed in September following what a Daewoo official described as unacceptable demands from the Europeans, including a buyback option. Frustrated, Daewoo put the hotel up for auction.

Kwek jumped in, joining 20 bids from a strong international field of 45 investors, including US investment bank Goldman Sachs and the Shangri-La Group. The field was whittled down to a dozen, but the buyers could smell Daewoo's blood and many came with conditions which the Koreans found hard to stomach. Among them was to remove the Hilton brand. Daewoo was not keen; they wanted to keep Seoul Hilton's name because the hotel had been associated with Daewoo for many years and it would be a face-saving measure for the disgraced group. In a Korean society where appearances were paramount, not preserving the name was a potential deal-breaker. In addition, Hilton had signed a management contract with Daewoo till 2003, meaning that the Koreans would have to compensate the chain if it was terminated prematurely.

The Singaporean knew instinctively that that was where he could gain an edge over the other potential buyers. "Daewoo was already in a lot of trouble and had so many problems, why did I want to make his life more difficult with lots of conditions?" he said. "They were in no mood or had no resources to handle this anymore. So I gave a very good and fair price and promised to keep Hilton. I told them 'I'll take it as it is'." Even though he had embarked on a rebranding exercise of all his hotels under the Millennium name, he was willing to give this latest one a miss. "It was still the early days of the Millennium brand, so nobody knew about it. Might as well have the old name which everybody knew," he said. "Maybe I could learn from Hilton?" Always practical, never dogmatic.

The Daewoo chairman also wanted to retain the penthouse in the hotel for him and his family, a condition which most other bidders found unacceptable. Kwek did not hesitate in agreeing to it, said his niece Patricia Yeo, who was leading discussions in Seoul. "He was so sure," she recalled. "There wasn't any element of doubt that he wanted this deal, and that it could be done. He kept telling me, 'Don't look at the small things, look at the big picture. What is this? It is a trophy asset. You'll never get a chance to do it again.'"

The Koreans chose him even though it was believed that his offer price was not the highest. In November 1999, he shelled out US$213.5 million to acquire the five-star Seoul Hilton. It was a hotel buy which would turn out to be his most profitable in his career, but more on that later. The acquisition added to his growing list of landmark hotels around the world. "It is very difficult, next to impossible, to buy a trophy hotel such as the Seoul Hilton. The opportunity came as a surprise," he said in 1999. "Such good opportunities hardly ever arise, such as The Plaza deal in New York. The Seoul Hilton reminds me of the Grand Hyatt Taipei, which is today the best-performing hotel in Asia within our group."

Kwek had successfully shrugged off the Asian Financial Crisis, and also a legal defeat which would ironically hamper his, well, millennium plans. CDL Hotels' push to use the Millennium brand name in Singapore was surprisingly thwarted by fellow Singapore developer Pontiac, which sued Kwek's outfit. Pontiac, under the Kwee family, argued in court that there would be confusion between the Millennium hotels and its own upcoming hotel, the Ritz-Carlton, Millenia Singapore.

The court ruled in favour of Pontiac in the midst of the recession, and banned CDL Hotels from using the name Millennium in all its hotels in Singapore. Kwek would switch to use the Copthorne brand instead, including with his prized King's Hotel. "Over time, your wounds heal to some extent. Of course it was irritating," he said. "I have hotels in five continents under my brand, but I can't use it in my own country. But we moved to brand hotels worldwide under Millennium," he said. "So in that sense, it didn't really affect us."

The episode was relegated to the footnotes of history as he waltzed into the new millennium at the top of the hotel world, almost exactly a decade after he began his global journey from King's to kingdom. He now owned 117 hotels around the world in 13 countries. In 2000, his peers paid him tribute as the Asian hotelier who had made the most impact on the international hotel industry in the 1990s, giving him the Asia Pacific Hotelier of the Decade award at the Third Annual Asia Pacific Hotel Investment Conference. When presenting the award to Kwek, the founder of the Regent hotel chain and Aman Resorts, Adrian Zecha, said: "What Kwek Leng Beng has achieved in the last 10 years is monumental. CDL Hotels is no longer an Asian hotel company, but a global one." Kwek replied in jest: "I'll have to work harder to reach the target of acquiring a major hotel chain in the next decade to win the award again."

It gave him great pride to be an ambassador of his country. "An American whom I met for the first time in London told me: 'In the US, people in the hotel industry are now saying things like, maybe Mr Kwek will buy this hotel chain, and don't rule him out. He may come out of all a sudden and grab it'," he said in an interview with *The Straits Times* in 2000. "I am glad the industry recognises what I am doing. I am proud because I come from such a little country like Singapore and I am able to impress them this way, not by words but by deeds."

His compatriots at home knew they had found a global champion. He was honoured as the 1996 Businessman of the Year in Singapore, with the citation saying: "In particular for his bold hotel acquisitions which have made CDL Hotels one of the world's largest hotel owners." And during the National Day Rally speech in 2001, the most important annual political address of the nation, then Prime Minister Goh Chok Tong singled out Kwek as an enterprising business leader who had turned his local family-run firm into an international Singapore company. "We need more...Kwek Leng Bengs," said Goh.

CHAPTER 14

Ground Zero

"This hotel is a symbol of what's in store for New York City, New York State and America as a whole. The best is yet to come for New York City."

— New York City mayor Michael Bloomberg during the 2003 reopening of the Millenium Hilton.

The moment the second plane crashed into the World Trade Center in New York on September 11 in 2001, Kwek Leng Beng knew the world he had lived in in the past 60 years would change forever. Travel would never be the same again, hospitality would be shaken at its roots and thick red lines would be drawn between civilisations. Business and development, especially his, would have to adapt to a brand new normal. What he did not bargain for was the possibility for tragedy to hit a lot closer to his home and heart.

His son, Sherman, was working out of an office in the Twin Towers. "I panicked," he said. "I was hunting high and low to see where he was, and I couldn't contact him." Thankfully, hours later, he got word that Sherman had switched to a new company in midtown Manhattan a few months earlier. Kwek thought his workplace was still in the World Trade Center. "Sometimes luck plays a part," he said.

A bullet dodged, but Kwek would not be as fortunate the next time. In the aftermath of both towers collapsing, American cable news networks began reporting that surrounding buildings were also in danger of crashing down. The façade of the nearby One Liberty Plaza had partially collapsed. The Deutsche Bank Building and the Verizon Building sustained significant damage and concerns were raised. But the biggest question mark was placed on the Millenium Hilton Hotel, which was across the street from the World Trade Center. "There was strong speculation that my hotel was going to collapse too," he said. "But there was so much confusion no one knew what was really going on."

Seven years after he bought his first hotel in the United States with the Millenium — wrong spelling and all — Kwek would be dealt his most serious blow in his hitherto unidirectional upward climb of building a global hotel empire. Not only was the Millenium at existential risk, but the September 11 cataclysm also posed serious threats to his worldwide portfolio of hotels given its impact on global tourism. As commentator Lee Han Shih observed in *The Business Times*: "If buying the Regal chain's US hotels in 1999 was the high point for developer-turned-hotelier Kwek Leng Beng, then the attack on the World Trade Center…must be his low point."

While Kwek was able to survive the Asian Financial Crisis

THE MILLENIUM HILTON

relatively unbothered partly because of his hotels in the West, the same gargantuan network of rooms would now put him squarely in the heart of Ground Zero. Three weeks after being feted by the Singapore Prime Minister at the National Day Rally, Kwek's world had come crashing down.

The crisis hit his team on the ground in Lower Manhattan immediately. Debris rained down in the Millenium "like confetti," described a restaurant manager. An announcement was quickly made over the hotel tannoy that a plane had flown into the World Trade Center and that guests should stay in their rooms because of the falling debris. When the second plane crashed into the Twin Towers, Millenium evacuated all guests. "We were ushered up the street into the general mayhem and for the first time in my life, I saw blood on the road along with shoes and someone's glasses. It was alarming," recalled British traveller Katherine Hardy in *Newsweek* magazine.

At the hotel lobby, human resources manager Ray Burgos grabbed a cart of clean laundry and handed out towels to the shell-shocked survivors streaming from across the World Trade Center. They asked for water. "But we didn't have enough water pitchers," Burgos told the *New York Times*. "So we dumped liquor out of the bottles in the lobby bar, filled them with water and gave them to people in need. One guy said: 'What kind of water is this? It tastes like Scotch!' He drank it anyway."

For many of the Millenium's staff, the feeling of déjà vu was unmistakable. It was a similar scene which they had confronted back in 1993, a year before Kwek bought the hotel, when a truck bomb was detonated by terrorists at the World Trade Center, killing six people and injuring over a thousand. The hotel's doorman, Kofi Myantakyi, told the *Times*: "I stared with disbelief as (the plane) moved right into that building. I saw the smoke. I thought, 'Just like 1993.' And then came the sirens. And that, too, was just like 1993."

Out on the streets in 2001, the staff and guests watched on in horror as people jumped from the World Trade Center. "When I saw the people jumping, I was praying to God," said hotel cleaner Leonard Williams. "And then they began hitting the wooden concert platform in the plaza, where I used to see the concerts they had. It was horrible. I cried like a baby."

The quick thinking of the Millenium management and staff ensured a swift evacuation of about 150 employees and 650 guests that morning of September 11. Not a single person was lost inside the hotel. But 12 guests who went to the Twin Towers never returned and are believed to have perished. No one was able to return to the hotel to retrieve their belongings for months. "When I saw the fire-trucks I assumed they would put out the fire and then we would go back to the hotel and everything would continue as normal. Of course, that didn't happen," said hotel guest Hardy.

What happened was that the 55-storey hotel suffered severe damage. Two-thirds of its glass front was shattered or broken. The building was covered in soot and ashes, blown out from across the road. There were massive toxic contaminants from the fire and collapse, recalled Kwek. "The hotel was pretty much blasted out in all intents and purposes," he said. "It was inhospitable." Millenium's then managing director Roger Swadish went back inside the hotel two days after the disaster and he told the *Times*: "I was in shock at first, to see the fire, the smoke, the damage to the hotel. We will have to take the entire hotel down to the drywall." In the words of John Wilson, the then chief executive of Millennium & Copthorne Hotels, "the building has sustained some unquantified damage."

There was much chatter in New York that the building structure was unsound. A *Bloomberg* report cited US law enforcement officials and firefighters who said several skyscrapers, including the Millenium, had suffered structural damage. Kwek faced much pressure to tear down the building. "New York City authorities approached us concerning building safety. But I wanted my own expert opinion before any decision was made. What was the basis for them saying that the Millenium was unsafe?" he said. "Let's not speculate. Let me bring in a world-renowned structural engineer and get an expert's view."

He personally invited Alfred Yee, one of the US' top structural engineers, to inspect his battered hotel. Yee was a civil engineer pioneer whose innovative designs of high-rise buildings survived high-intensity earthquakes across the Pacific Rim. "He was the best in the business I have ever come across," said Kwek, who had earlier enlisted Yee's services when building Republic Plaza. "And he convinced me that my hotel was safe. He also convinced New York City officials, and convinced Hilton because they were managing the hotel and they wouldn't manage a hotel if the building was unsafe."

Kwek decided to rebuild, costs notwithstanding. "September 11 is a tragedy which the world will never forget," he said. "I want to rebuild this hotel to show the world that we won't be defeated. I will rebuild a landmark and an icon as a symbol to remember the tragedy." It was a mammoth task. Some 80 per cent of the interior had to be replaced. "As the owner of the hotel, we had to work with Hilton, the operator, to manage the restoration of the hotel," he added. "Luckily the hotel was solid and structures intact. We had to deal with architects, designers, contractors, insurance companies, unions, government authorities. Those were difficult times after such a catastrophic event."

To make it worse, the other parts of his business were floundering. After the terrorist attacks, City Developments Limited (CDL) shares fell 38 per cent, the lowest level since October 1998 during the Asian Financial Crisis. Occupancy rates for the company's other hotels in New York City dropped by almost 70 per cent in the aftermath. There were strong global fears of a sharp decline in business and leisure travels, devastating tourism, hotel and aviation. Kwek moved to allay investors' fears after a heavy sell-down, sharing plans to pivot to US domestic travellers, cap investment in hotels and even dispose of some non-core hotels.

But to make matters even worse, problems soon arose with the insurers over the damage suffered by the hotel. The Millenium was insured for US$310 million and the payout would fund the rebuilding and the loss of business. CDL claimed US$108.8 million from insurance company Travelers, including property damage of US$33.6 million, business interruption losses of US$74 million and other expenses of US$1.2 million. After advancing US$46.5 million to CDL, Travelers refused to pay more. It sued CDL in 2003, arguing that it was not obligated to pay business interruption losses on the Millenium. CDL made a counterclaim. "It was David versus Goliath," said Kwek. "And make no mistake, I was the David. Travelers was a US$100-billion company."

The trouble did not hold back CDL from rebuilding the Millenium. In March 2003, 18 months after the disaster, it reopened to much fanfare after a US$32-million renovation makeover. Every room now had a plasma screen television, cordless phone and high-speed Internet access — all the new must-haves for business travellers. The hotel was "literally brand new," said CDL in a media release, with refurbishments from the penthouse to the lobby. It would boast the full suite of amenities, including a business centre, indoor heated pool, fitness centre, on-site parking and 24-hour room service. At its opening, graced by New York City mayor Michael Bloomberg and New York State governor George Pataki, and joined by firemen and union officials, a parade was held to celebrate the return of a Lower Manhattan icon.

However, there was still no resolution on the insurance claims. There were almost "daily fights," with the insurance company, he revealed. He tried to settle the suit privately and after repeated rounds of failure, both sides eventually gathered at Kwek's Millennium Hotel Broadway Times Square for one final attempt in December 2004 before the battle went to the courts. Both sides hired top American lawyers from New York firms, and despite repeated presentations and arguments, no one was willing to back down. "I was in a big conference room with all my lawyers, and the other side was in another room with their lawyers," he recalled. "When my side said something, the arbitrator would take it and bring to the other side. A few hours later, he would return with their reply. This went on and on." Meanwhile, the lawyers clocked in their hours, with the bill sent to CDL. By the second day, Kwek had had enough.

He asked his lawyers if he could speak to the arbitrator. His lawyers demurred, saying that it was unusual — the communication was usually left to the lawyers. "I told them that I could make a decision now. I wanted to speak to somebody on the other side who could also make a decision, with the arbitrator present," he said. When the meeting was finally set up with his opposite counterpart, the Singaporean wasted no time in getting to the heart of the matter. "I told the other guy 'You think your case is very strong because your lawyers tell you it is very strong'," he said. "'Well, my lawyers also tell me that my case is very strong. Actually, both our cases are not very strong. So let's be practical and reasonable. You cannot say you won't pay me anything. Can we meet somewhere in between?'" Within minutes, they shook hands on a settlement of US$25 million, down from about US$60 million claimed by CDL. "I told him 'Let's stop fighting, let's go home, let's bring this back as a Christmas present'."

Under the terms of settlement, both parties dropped all related litigation. "I'm a person who doesn't like to depend on lawyers or civil servants. I'm my own man. So I decided, and that's it!" he said. "I didn't want to continue fighting with Travelers. They were so big, what's the point of arguing all the time? I'm a practical man, with a practical solution. Everybody's happy. Case closed."

More than three years after September 11, Kwek could finally close the book on this tragedy and loss. As he once said when looking back on this incident: "Hospitality is not all handshakes and good food." But with more than a bit of grit, he managed to rebound. And as he had predicted, his hotel, now named Millennium Downtown New York Hotel, has become the go-to place for travellers who want to visit Ground Zero, or the memorial museum today. The site is visible from more than three-quarters of the rooms and the restaurant in the hotel. "I was not afraid. I know New York is the most resilient city in the US," he said. "People are tough and resilient in New York." The same could be said for him.

citi

Part 5

The Great Southern Strategy

”

I wanted to do something that nobody had done before, so that I had no competitor.

— Kwek Leng Beng

CHAPTER 15

The Sail Worth Waiting For

"Hats off to Mr Kwek for seeing that there would be demand for waterfront living in the city centre and that rich foreigners would buy into an iconic development."

— **The Business Times** *in 2005.*

The new millennium had not been kind to Kwek Leng Beng. The dot.com crash in 2000 was exacerbated by the September 11 attacks the next year, dealing two severe blows to the global economy, particularly in the United States. His hotel empire was reeling. To make it worse, the real estate market in Asia remained in absolute doldrums, struggling to exit a long winter which began with the Asian Financial Crisis in 1997. When City Developments (CDL) announced its results for financial year ending 2001, it was an ugly sight. Its net profit had plunged 85.5 per cent to S$41.6 million.

Kwek badly needed a turnaround and he would find it in an unlikely project at home, kickstarting a great southern strategy which would allow him to dominate the coastline of Singapore over the next decade. The opening came in what was known in the property sector as the government's "reserve list." In layman speak, it allowed the market to trigger land sales by putting in a bid that the government was willing to accept. CDL's rival Pontiac Land Group activated the reserve list for a plot of land in Marina Bay, earmarked by the authorities as the New Downtown to supplement the congested neighbouring Shenton Way. The trigger brought the site into an open public tender in March 2002 and Kwek decided to join the race.

But sensing that the market remained very subdued, he reckoned Pontiac would not dramatically increase its original bid of S$280 million. What he and his CDL team did not expect was that the economy was so lacklustre that there were no other bidders except Pontiac and them, said CDL group general manager Chia Ngiang Hong. "We were surprised that we were the only tender besides the original one," he said. When the results were announced two months later in May, the market was stunned that CDL had won with a bid of S$288.9 million, while Pontiac stuck to its price of S$280 million. Kwek had won with a bid that was only 3 per cent higher. The schadenfreude was unmistakable. Four years after losing the legal bid to use the Millennium hotel brand in Singapore to Pontiac, Kwek had cocked a snook to the Kwees, said senior CDL executives. "He didn't say it, but we could tell he was very pleased to beat Pontiac by only 3 per cent," said Hong Leong Group spokesman Gerry De Silva.

CDL had scored a big bargain. Its bid of S$227 per square foot (psf) per plot ratio (ppr) was also much lower than the S$290 psf ppr price that a Keppel Land-led consortium paid the previous year for a bigger adjacent site, which has since been developed into the Marina Bay Financial Centre (MBFC). But after the cheers of winning came the conundrum of development. "After we got the site, the headache came," recalled Chia. "What to do with the site? Office? Retail? Hotel? There was a big debate." Unlike most real estate in Singapore, the Marina Bay plot of land was categorised by the authorities as a "white site." That meant the developer could put it to commercial, residential or hotel use, or a mix of these.

Given the location in the Central Business District (CBD), the immediate and obvious choice would be to build offices. And Kwek went down the route briefly, even negotiating with Standard Chartered to buy an office tower when completed. Unfortunately, or fortunately as the story goes, the bank could not seek a favourable release from its existing landlord, and the deal died. CDL relooked its options and Kwek realised that going commercial was too cookie-cutter in the area. There was already a glut of offices and with the new MBFC emerging with three office towers, supply was in abundance.

To give CDL the millennium fillip it was screaming for, he needed a more edgy project that would seize imaginations. He decided to go with residential, experimenting with Singapore's first major condominium in the CBD. It would be waterfront living, offering an expansive view of the sea. "I wanted to do something that nobody had done before, so that I had no competitor," he said. "I would be the first pioneer and everybody would clap." Alas, not everyone did — at least not initially. Chia revealed that a CDL director was openly apprehensive about the move. "He said 'Are you sure you can sell homes in CBD? No one has done it, you know?'," recalled Chia with a laugh. "There were a lot of sceptics because the whole area was quite empty. The casino was not even announced yet!" Kwek heard the naysayers. "People told me there was nothing to do in CBD," he said. "So I came up with the slogan — Live, Work, Play."

Not only did he ignore the dissenting voices, but he even doubled down on his decision. CDL commissioned award-winning Norwegian-American architect Peter Pran to build a two-tower 245m-high condominium that would be the tallest residential building in Singapore, the seventh highest in Asia and the 10th highest in the world. At 1,111 units, it was also the biggest residential project that Kwek and CDL had undertaken. Shaped like a sail, it aimed to be a landmark to anchor Marina Bay and demonstrate Singapore's position as a lighthouse to a vibrant Asia. Pran said that he was "trying to create a feeling of how it'd be like to live at the top of a sail mast, where you're suspended in space, taking in the magnificent panorama of Singapore and the sea." It was named The Sail @ Marina Bay. Kwek was not just trying to prove the cynics wrong. He wanted to shout from the top of the world.

Succeed, and The Sail would be a gateway statement of intent for

CDL and by extension Kwek. Fail, and it would be the most visible laughing stock in the gleaming Singapore skyline. While Kwek said in several interviews for this book that he was not a gambler, he played for high stakes this time. And as he crossed into 2003, it seemed as though the odds would not be in his favour. In March, the SARS epidemic broke out in Singapore and across Asia. The already weak property market suffered a severe setback, putting a major dent into Kwek's flagship project. "The market was quite quiet then, and demand very uncertain," said Chia. "The boss himself was quite anxious."

As the mysterious virus outbreak receded and The Sail was prepped for a soft launch in late 2004, CDL decided that it would need a robust marketing strategy. "We thought we needed a big bang to drum up interest," said Chia. Instead of a regular show flat, the company rented the Customs House at Clifford Pier by the sea, so as to replicate, as much as possible, the sea view that residents would be able to enjoy. To top it off, there was a launch at the nearby Merlion — the tourism icon of Singapore — with fireworks on water, fanfare and music. Then, just to be sure, Kwek appointed himself informal chief marketing officer of The Sail, calling up contacts and urging them to buy units. He made the pitch that went beyond its 24-hour concierge service, fully-equipped spa with café and therapy room. "I told everyone that this was a very unique project, one of its kind. The prices were very cheap, and they would definitely make money. Must buy!" he said. To show his personal commitment to the project, he bought four units. Chia recalled with a chuckle: "Whoever he saw, he would ask them to buy. He was personally marketing for us."

It worked. When The Sail, which was a joint venture with insurance giant AIA, launched its first tower in November 2004 at an average price of about S$900 psf, demand was brisk. About 350 units out of 681 were sold in the opening weeks, with some buyers even buying whole floors of the 99-year leasehold development. When buyers wanted one of the four penthouses available, Kwek even gave up the unit he had reserved. "I looked at it from a business point of view," he told the media.

He felt that the demand signposted the beginning of an upturn in Singapore's real estate after seven years. "To me, as an investor or a property man who reads the market — just like I sold The Plaza in New York at the best price — I think this (Singapore residential) market is just recovering," he said then. He would follow up six months later in mid-2005 by declaring publicly that property prices in Singapore would go up by 20 to 30 per cent in the next two to three years. The local media was sceptical, with a daily running a caricature of Kwek blowing hot air.

Kwek would be proven right almost right away. In late 2005, CDL launched the second tower of The Sail, soon after the government announced the building of an integrated resort at Marina Bay. There was a queue overnight to grab choice units. When doors opened at the showflat, there was a near stampede and a security guard fainted amid the human rush. Afternoon tabloid *The New Paper* said that "it's a scene that hasn't been seen in Singapore for some time." CDL initially launched 100 units in Tower Two, but quickly released another 170 units given the overwhelming demand. By the end of the day, almost all 270 units were sold. This despite prices rising to S$1,200 psf, a sharp spike from the first tower released a year earlier. Kwek knew his fellow Singaporeans' herd mentality well. "In the beginning, of course, it is always difficult," he said. "But, after a while, as everybody rushes to buy, a Singaporean cannot be left out. There is a psychology; we played into the psychology."

The craze over The Sail was the clearest indication that the property market was trending up, especially in the high-end residential sector. It put an end to what an observer in Singapore described as "seven years of famine in the Singapore private residential property market." The Sail was the lighthouse which lit the turning point, said Chia. "With The Sail and the integrated resort, everything picked up after that. Whoever bought the units made tons of money! There were lots of very, very happy people."

The happiest though was the man who decided to build homes where offices stood, turning an experiment into an emblem. "At that time, I had no idea the government was going to put an integrated resort in Marina Bay, but it's my instinct that this project would work," said Kwek. "The Sail is my most iconic residential project and the one which I'm most proud of." He would soon cast his eyes towards the sea at the next icon of Singapore.

Chapter 16

The Forgotten Man of Marina Bay Sands

"It's a mark of secure strength that for him, the satisfaction is having done it rather than the idea of advertising his role."

— architect Moshe Safdie.

When Singapore Prime Minister Lee Hsien Loong announced in August 2004 that his government would consider breaking decades-old taboo to build a casino, reactions from the society were a volatile cocktail of excitement, concern and outright fear. But there were no such mixed feelings for Kwek Leng Beng. He knew immediately that it was the right decision to reinvent the country's economy and image, a change which could fundamentally alter Singapore's global reputation. While some demurred publicly on grounds of morals and mores, he openly plumped for it. "Singapore must move with the times. We should nurture a mindset change," he told the local media in the weeks after the news. In good measure, he suggested where the landmark casino ought to be built — on the empty reclaimed Marina Bay which The Sail looked out to.

Of course, given his track record, he was never going to stay on the sidelines as an observer for long. When the government made public that Singapore was going to build not one, but two, integrated resorts (IR) with casinos, Kwek and City Developments Limited (CDL) quickly emerged as potential bidders for the projects. But he had only eyes for the Marina Bay development, distancing himself from the parallel project in tourism island Sentosa. Given the Marina Bay site's stated focus on conventions and hotel businesses by the authorities, CDL felt it was more compatible with its businesses.

As word on the street stirred that a winning bid should ideally be a joint venture between a global gaming player and a local property company, Kwek began to be courted by some of the biggest names in the casino business. Yet, as MGM Mirage tied up with CapitaLand and Harrah's Entertainment partnered Keppel Land — both government-linked real estate giants — the Kwek camp remained noncommittal. Even when 19 bids were submitted in early 2005 for the two sites in an initial request for concepts, CDL was nowhere to be seen. "We have not submitted any plan at all," Kwek told the media in March 2005, at CDL's full-year financial results briefing. "We've been approached by almost all the international players, including the regional ones. We have adopted a position not to tie up at this stage because if you tie up with A company and A company doesn't get it, then what is your position? It's better for us to be on the side, then if anybody gets it, then (if) they want to negotiate, we will negotiate. If the terms are correct, we will go in with them; if the terms are not, then we don't go in and say goodbye."

Truth was, as he revealed in an interview for this book, none of the suitors had impressed him. Some were insincere, others did not seem reliable, most were simply not bad but also not that good. When asked to share their concepts for the integrated resorts, Kwek found designs which were aesthetically pleasing but wholly impractical. "They gave me beautiful presentations with designs which were fanciful, but without concrete substance. Yes, they looked very nice. But how can it help the economy?" he recalled. He was unmoved by the proposals for Cirque du Soleil or other entertainment attractions. "Some of the things disclosed by other contenders, as a businessman, I think that some of the things are nothing... It's a question of writing out a cheque," he said in 2006. For a man who has said on occasions that he does not marry easily, he quipped in public during the tender process that it was good to "get to know as many girls as possible before you get engaged."

Soon, the boy would meet the boy of his dreams. When Sheldon Adelson, the boss of Las Vegas Sands, came a-calling, Kwek found a kindred spirit in the gaming tycoon. The Singaporean liked that the American was going to sink billions of his own net worth into Sands' eventual US$6.88 billion investment, through his more than 60 per cent stake in Sands. That spoke to Kwek's heart, who likened it to his own stake in his hotel arm, Millennium & Copthorne

(M&C): "I control 53 per cent of M&C. Every pound it loses, I lose 53 cents. So whatever I want to do, I must have confidence and make sure I can make money." This, to him, distinguished Adelson from the other bidders. "That's the difference between an entrepreneur and a professional," said Kwek in a media interview in 2006. "How many have the confidence to put their money where their mouth is?"

It did not matter that the mouth belonged to the famously abrasive and often cantankerous Adelson. Kwek enjoyed sparring and working with a near mirror image of himself. Sands' man on the ground in Singapore then, George Tanasijevich, said the pair of giants had a very comfortable fit. "They very quickly formed a strong relationship and a meaningful friendship," he shared. When he wanted to visit Sands in Las Vegas, Adelson sent his private jet to fetch the Singaporean. Kwek liked what Sands was proposing for Marina Bay — mega conventions. "Of all the proposals I had seen, his business model was the one which I believed would benefit Singapore the most," he said. "I saw his conventions in Vegas, his massive shopping malls. If Singapore could have something like that, it would be fantastic. That's when I decided to work with him." When he returned to Singapore, he told his spokesman Gerry De Silva that Sands was "really big." "I was quite amused that this big tycoon of Asia was impressed with someone much larger than him," said De Silva.

For Sands and Adelson, the affection was mutual. "The

engagement that we had with Chairman Kwek and CDL was really quite seamless, and came together rather quickly," said Tanasijevich. "And we really were pretty much singularly focused on them after some initial discussions with various local companies." After months of talk, Adelson met Kwek in his Chinese restaurant Hua Ting in Orchard Hotel in Singapore, and the pair sealed the deal over dinner. Kwek said he shared "the same wavelength" as Adelson. "We are practical people," he said in 2006. "We are not there to talk about theories like university undergrads or scholars. We are there to say: this is workable, this is not workable. Let's not waste our time."

They agreed for CDL to take a 15 per cent stake in Sands' bid, and when the partnership was announced in December 2005, it immediately catapulted the team into frontrunner status, ahead of four others still in the running, including MGM Grand–CapitaLand and Harrah's–Keppel Land. The other two consortiums were Genting International and Star Cruises, and Australia's Publishing & Broadcasting and Melco International. Kwek and Adelson laid out their nascent bromance in public. The Singaporean said: "'If anyone can develop a successful IR of international appeal, it is Las Vegas Sands. I believe Sands sees us as adding value, given our extensive and valuable experience in property and hotels." The American returned the compliments: "The addition of City Developments to our Singapore team exemplifies our efforts to assemble the perfect combination of leading local and international talent needed to build and operate a successful world-class integrated resort." Market watchers agreed they were a formidable combination. A gaming analyst told *The Straits Times*: "Sands is the best foreign operator in Macau. It knows more about the China market than any of the other US gaming companies. It can bring so much to Singapore." Add to it the Kwek family, which has "this innate ability to read the Singapore market," and the contenders ought to be concerned about this new pairing.

Kwek went to work immediately, said Tanasijevich, giving the local inputs which Sands were craving for. "He was very straightforward, honest, capable, experienced, knowledgeable, and had very good instincts in terms of design and programming of the IR. He really understood what the role of the IR at Marina Bay was going to be, how it fit into the broader picture for government strategy on tourism or the URA master planning for that part of Singapore," he said, referring to the Urban Redevelopment Authority. "And of course, he knew everybody within the government that was playing a meaningful role in the process, and was able to give us insights as to how best to engage and what to prioritise, and what he thought would work versus what wouldn't work. And so it was a very, very fruitful relationship for us. He had great insights on Singapore, and was able to read between the lines."

Kwek urged Sands to up its number of rooms from 800 to over 2,500. Adelson agreed. Kwek pushed for renowned architect Moshe Safdie to step in to replace Sands' earlier choice. He was not impressed by the earlier design of skyscrapers against the coastline, obscuring the resort's seafront view. Adelson also agreed. The Singaporean said in 2006: "Moshe Safdie is an excellent choice as he has a deep understanding of Singapore's landscape and the government's master plan for Singapore." The Boston-based architect had already designed three projects in Singapore: the Ardmore Habitat condominiums, The Edge On Cairnhill and Simpang New Town.

Kwek, who had strong views on design, then paid close attention to the drawings and models of Safdie, beyond convincing Adelson to keep the SkyPark. He brought an Asian sensibility to the table, observed Tanasijevich. An earlier version of Safdie's design had the SkyPark symmetrical with both ends having a cantilever. Kwek and a *fengshui* master thought it was a bad idea, saying that it resembled a *torii*, a traditional Japanese gate often found at the entrance to a Shinto shrine. Given Asia's tragic memories of World War II and Singapore's brutal occupation by Japan, the cultural insensitivities would be highly controversial. "The feedback from Kwek and the *fengshui* master was that such imagery of that silhouette was not proper," said Tanasijevich. Safdie took the comments onboard, got rid of the cantilever at one end and pushed the SkyPark 67m past Tower One. It laid claim to the biggest cantilever in the world. "I liked it a lot because it made it very dynamic," said Safdie. Perhaps unintentionally, the futuristic ship-like behemoth in the sky became the perfect architectural maritime neighbour to Kwek's The Sail across the Marina Barrage.

The marriage of Vegas glitz and Singapore grit looked like a union made in business heaven. But just as the Sands–CDL shock and awe courtship had taken the market by surprise, its sudden divorce was almost as unexpected. Exactly a month after inking the deal with Adelson, Kwek stunned the world in January 2006 by announcing CDL was pulling out. CDL's official reasons were cryptic, citing only in a statement "some requirements associated with the bid." The tycoon would later elaborate that they quit because of regulatory restrictions and that some in CDL were unwilling to disclose their full financial background. "We clarified the rules and regulations, and we know it is impossible for us to comply, so we pulled out," he told *The Business Times*.

CDL was told by Sands that the checks were limited only to CDL, and not the hundreds of partnerships it was involved in. Sands president Bill Weidner would later express regret publicly. "We felt, to a certain extent, that we had let Leng Beng down. We took our regulatory experience and our experience in our marketplace, and we compared it to what happened in New Jersey, Nevada. But Singapore went beyond what we have experienced," he said. The amount of information required was believed to be staggering. To obtain a gaming licence in the United States and Australia, applicants must reveal their debts, mortgages, stocks, mutual funds, options, bonds, bank accounts, properties, tax filings, and not to mention financial, employment and legal history. This extends to spouses and children of the applicants too, leading some to joke that the checks are closer to a "strip show."

The local media speculated Kwek probably reckoned it was not worth it to give up so much for a 15 per cent stake. "As Singapore investigators continue probity checks on bidders for the Marina Bay integrated resort, they are likely to follow the same path in making sure no stone is left unturned," wrote *The Business Times*. "So it's little wonder that wealthy, privacy-conscious Asians — such as City Developments' Kwek Leng Beng — could baulk at such an intrusion and ultimately stay out of an IR bid."

But that was only half the story. The other half was tucked in a little clue in CDL's statement upon withdrawal. It said that the company and in particular Kwek would remain as an adviser to Sands' bid, but took pains to stress that the Singapore company's involvement was on the "non-gaming aspects." CDL would provide help and advice on "design, development and construction planning, as well as knowledge of the local market." Kwek shared in interviews for this book that he had to withdraw because of family objections. "Many members of my family didn't like for us to be involved in gaming and gambling," he said. "They felt it was not suitable for the family." His wife confirmed it. The devout Catholic revealed: "I said no no no, you cannot partner a casino."

The sudden pull out was seen as a severe blow to Sands' chances for the resort prize. Without a local partner who would plough gambling earnings back into Singapore, the hitherto frontrunner was not looking so attractive anymore. "There were no hard feelings, of course, but it did cause me some concern," said Tanasijevich. "In the absence of a local equity partner, that might not be viewed favourably by those who were going to make a decision."

But amid the exit commotion, few paid much attention to Kwek saying that he would stay on to help Sands' bid. Many dismissed it as a face-saving gesture. He would prove them very wrong. For the next three months, he worked behind the scenes with Safdie to refine the architecture and design, deeply aware that the authorities wanted an iconic building on the Marina Bay to anchor the city's skyline. On the eve of Sands' final pitch to a ministerial panel in Singapore, Kwek even gave a rare three-hour media interview over lunch, backing Adelson and Sands to the hilt. He stressed that the mega conventions model was the best bet to bring in high-spending business visitors, ideal for a mature tourism destination like Singapore. The next day, he joined the Sands delegation to do a 75-minute presentation to the ministerial panel. As Tanasijevich observed: "So, you know, it's not as if they exited the project at that time, it's just that they decided that they weren't going to be an equity partner."

The rather selfless act befuddled many, who wondered what Kwek stood to gain when he no longer had skin in the game. He told reporters in 2006: "You can ask the question why I am interested to help them when I have no financial interest in the project. The reason is very simple: I love Singapore. I want to see Singapore with an IR that is a success." He took a long and macro view, he elaborated in interviews for this book. "If this project is successful, the economy would pick up and everybody would benefit, including me. More tourists would come and the hotel business would improve. I'm not a businessman who thinks only about myself and ignores everyone else. I want to help to develop our economy. I don't want it to be stagnant." It was a stance he had consistently embraced in his career, shared Singapore's former Trade and Industry Minister George Yeo. "He took a broader view for the industry," he said. "It was never from a narrow self-interested point of view. He was never lobbying for his project or anything like that. Never."

Despite the twists and turns, Sands' bid prevailed. In May 2006, the Singapore government announced that it had snagged the most desired crown jewel in the global gaming industry. A call was quickly made to Kwek, who received the good news while stuck in a traffic jam in Bangkok, on his way to a press conference to open the Millennium Hilton Bangkok. Weidner was quick to pay tribute to CDL and Kwek, even though they had pulled out as a shareholder. "Together with the valuable insights of City Developments and its executive chairman, Kwek Leng Beng, and the strength of our in-house construction management team, we will create South-east Asia's No. 1 integrated resort that will inspire Singaporeans and draw visitors from overseas," he told the media.

And with that, Kwek's role behind what would come to be known around the world as Marina Bay Sands faded into private memories of a few and dusty newspaper archives. Many, including in Singapore, had long forgotten, or did not know, the role he had played in the country's new undisputed architectural icon. When the resort opened in 2010, there was nary a mention of the Singaporean. It did not bother him one bit. "Why do I want to let people know? Publicise? I want to be practical. I could help the economy. I'm very thankful, that's all."

Chapter 17

The Great Recession

> *"When the crisis hit, the partners had no money. Or even if they had money, they didn't want to put it into this project. So they made our lives very difficult."*
>
> ***— CDL group general manager Chia Ngiang Hong.***

It felt like the circle of life that Kwek Leng Beng would have to return to Beach Road at some point. Nearly seven decades after his father had started Hong Leong as a general trading company with a shopfront by the southern shores of Singapore, Kwek would gaze down at a majestic empty plot of land from a neighbouring building on the same road. "You have to tender for it," said real estate consultant and friend Edmund Tie, who was hosting Kwek in his office in Shaw Tower. Kwek knew he was right. While the location had long lost the relevance of its name because of Singapore's rapid land reclamation, it was still a superb piece of real estate. To its north, on the other side of Beach Road, was the iconic Raffles Hotel. On the other flank, across Nicoll Highway, sat Suntec City, one of the country's biggest shopping malls and convention centres. Property analysts went so far as to describe it as "the last iconic site in Singapore."

It whetted Kwek's appetite, a man with an eye for icons and a desire to build landmarks. This new site would be a fine addition to his string of pearls across the new waterfront of his hometown, from The Sail through Sentosa to Beach Road, glancing through the Marina Bay Sands (MBS) which he had so proudly been a part of, albeit fleetingly. The coup de grace in his Great Southern Strategy. But this beauty was too much to be owned by one man, or to be exact, one company. At a gross floor area of 146,827 square metres, the 99-year leasehold development was too big for City Developments Limited (CDL) to take on by itself. The integrated development, which had to include hotel rooms, offices, residential apartments and commercial shops, needed a consortium.

Kwek would find his among the most unlikely candidates. First, he approached the Israeli real estate firm El-Ad which had bought the Plaza Hotel from him three years earlier in 2004. They were keen. And in a move which surprised the world, he found a second partner in Dubai World, an investment company of the Dubai government in the United Arab Emirates. Just as he had played interlocutor between Prince Alwaleed bin Talal and El-Ad in the Plaza sale, Kwek would prove once again that it was no fluke that he could bridge Arab-Israeli interests in a manner which few in the world could pull off. "I should win a Nobel Peace Prize," he joked.

What he did not realise was that he was so good at his peacekeeping job that the Arabs and Israelis would eventually gang up against him! But more on that later. The unlikely three-way consortium put in a strong proposal in July 2007, designed to win a two-envelope bidding system. That meant the Urban Redevelopment Authority of Singapore (URA) would choose to evaluate the concepts before looking at the bidding price. A poor design would be struck off in the first envelope, without even reaching the second, which would reveal the money to be tabled. Kwek, who had participated in a similar tender process with MBS, knew that the authorities meant what they had promised. He had to put in a winning design. Price was to come later.

Moshe Safdie was considered as architect, and he revealed that he was keen on the project. But CDL's group general manager Chia Ngiang Hong said that Kwek decided it was better to let Safdie focus on MBS. Such was his passion for the project even though he was no longer a part of the integrated resort. Instead, Kwek chose British architect Norman Foster, who was drawing plenty of attention in this part of the world for his soon-to-be-unveiled Beijing airport, the signature architecture in China's welcome party to the 2008 Summer Olympics.

Foster and team's design was a breakthrough with green features such as slanting cutting-edge façades to catch winds and direct air flow to the ground, collecting water from the towers to an underground tank, and a solar system that maximised sun radiation which would power the façade lightings. The centrepiece was a 280m-long microclimatic canopy which would not only provide shade, but also collect rainwater for landscape irrigation, incorporate solar panels for renewable energy and integrate the two new towers with the heritage buildings. Part of the URA requirements for the project was that the design had to blend and connect four conservation blocks which were part of the old Beach Road army camp. Modernity in sync with the environment, and perfectly in step with the heritage flavour of the venue. The location was the site of the first National Service enlistment in Singapore in 1967, the beginning of conscription in the then young nation.

Kwek got his calculations and bearings perfectly, playing the two-envelope system with a geometric precision that would make a mathematician proud. As his life circled back to Beach Road, he knew exactly how to shape his strategy. Of the seven bids submitted, five did not make it to the second stage. They included joint ventures by Pontiac Land Group and Morgan Stanley; Keppel Land and Cheung Kong Holdings; CapitaLand; and two bids by Overseas Union Enterprise. Only the consortium led by CDL and another joint venture between Keppel Land and Cheung Kong Holdings progressed to the second envelope where the tender was to be awarded to the higher bidder. The Keppel Land–Cheung Kong Holdings bid was S$1.39 billion. CDL consortium's S$1.69 billion was comfortably higher. It translated into S$1,069 per square foot of potential gross floor area.

It was euphoria for CDL, its partners and Kwek. URA praised the concept proposal as a "compelling and attractive scheme," that would lead to a "truly distinctive development and an exemplary showcase of 'green' architecture in Singapore." The development, to be called The South Beach, will become a "revolutionary New Eco-Quarter in Singapore," when it is completed, said CDL with more than a bit of hyperbole amid the excitement. Even Kwek could not resist a bit of braggadocio: "We are confident that The South Beach will elevate Singapore's unique branding as a global city and help attract more prominent investors from all over the world."

But the happiness did not last very long. Almost as soon as the results were announced, the losing bidders made known their dissatisfaction with CDL's victory. It led *The Business Times* to run a story headlined "Size of winning bid colours green project." In it, the report said: "As a new symbol of environmentally-friendly architecture was unveiled yesterday, green became the topic of discussion in more ways than one. The award of the former NCO Club/Beach Road camp grounds to a City Developments consortium was accompanied by a tinge of envy as observers pointed out that the winning land bid of nearly S$1.69 billion is believed to be around S$500 million lower than the top bid, which was not even shortlisted under the two-envelope tender." Market chatter said that the highest bid was more than S$2 billion, and those who missed out voiced their displeasure openly through unofficial channels, said Chia. "There were a lot of unhappy people who said they bid half a billion higher than us and still lost," he recalled. "Quite a big hoo-ha. But as far as we were concerned, we were the winner on design and price. Singapore's system is very transparent. Once decided, you can't step back. This project had some controversy from the start."

Whatever snide remarks from the outside paled in comparison to the trouble that would soon erupt internally between the three consortium partners. When the subprime mortgage crisis eventually led to the fall of Lehman Brothers in September 2008, two of the three legs in the South Beach consortium collapsed. El-Ad, which was based in the United States, was heavily exposed to the American economy and property market. It wanted a way out of the project. By late 2009, Dubai World was in deep financial trouble too, and the market was flooded with talk that they wanted to exit The South Beach as well. "When the crisis hit, the partners had no money," said Chia. "Or even if they had money, they didn't want to put it into this project. So they made our lives very difficult."

Kwek's nephew, Eik Sheng, the son of his late younger brother Leng Joo, just joined the family business then and remembered a rough start. He said: "It was really tough for CDL back then, because both of them were being very difficult with us and they didn't want to put in any money." Both parties also set aside any geopolitical differences there might have been and went on the offensive towards CDL. "They told us to reduce construction costs and talk to the banks to get higher financing for the project," added Kwek Eik Sheng. "They said 'don't ask us for more money'." Soon both El-Ad and Dubai World blamed CDL for not managing the project well. "It was acrimonious; it was both of them against us and we couldn't get the project moving. A lot of decisions were stuck," said Kwek

Eik Sheng. "As the local partner, it was our reputation in Singapore at stake. We learnt quite a lot of lessons from this."

At times, the relationships degenerated into pure shouting matches between Kwek Leng Beng and the Israelis and Arabs, revealed CDL senior staff. "There was a lot of fighting during the board meetings," said Chia. "The chairman was very insistent that they had to do certain things and that they could not drag the project down. During some meetings, the chairman even screamed at them. He was very steady and insistent and wouldn't give way easily. He had many arguments and he really told them off. Very loud. He wanted to do it right for the project. There was tension because the crisis sucked up all the money. But when they got no money, they just got desperate."

While CDL had first right of refusal as joint venture partners, the price had to be right, said Kwek in an interview with the media in December 2009. "I have heard rumours circulating that one or both of them may want to get out. If they do want to get out, obviously they will come to us first and offer us," he said. "In fact, we have tested and asked whether they want to get out. They want to get out at a profit, I say good bye. Some of them will want to get out. Some of them will just want to carry on because (they) are looking at it on a longer-term basis. You cannot look at this kind of project — which will take four to five years — and say I am not interested because the market has turned. You (have to) look at it in the medium to longer term if you believe there is a future in Singapore." The construction of The South Beach, which was originally slated to be completed in 2012, had to be delayed. CDL announced a deferment in late 2008, saying works would begin after construction costs had eased.

Meanwhile, Kwek had to also fight fire on the Hong Leong Finance (HLF) front. His company had been the single biggest seller of toxic Lehman-linked products in Singapore, leading to a seven-month investigation by the Monetary Authority of Singapore (MAS). HLF had sold a total of S$106.2 million worth of Minibond and Pinnacle structured notes to 2,781 investors, of which 428 had no prior investment experience. MAS slapped HLF with a two-year sanction from selling structured notes, which was the most severe ban among the 10 financial institutions in Singapore. In an HLF meeting to deal with the crisis, president Ian MacDonald recalled Kwek "bouncing up" the spiral staircase, eager to interview the ones who had sold the products. "He wanted very much to solve the problem," said MacDonald. "He had a long-term view, and it was never to sweep the problems under the carpet."

Kwek decided that HLF would pay the most in compensation in Singapore, some S$57.6 million in total — which worked out to full or partial compensation for 95.5 per cent of the cases. He also sued Morgan Stanley in New York in 2012, accusing the Wall Street investment bank of fraudulently selling Hong Leong investment products that were designed to fail. "He took the line very quickly that we couldn't allow a big bank to bully us," said former HLF group financial controller Soon Yee Christie. HLF said in its complaint that it was "an unwitting victim of Morgan Stanley's scheme." The Singapore company failed in its lawsuit, with the US court dismissing the claims a year later because of a lack of jurisdiction due to HLF not having any business or clients in the US.

At South Beach, the impasse continued with the two partners both unwilling to put in funds to get the construction started. In mid-2009, the project secured a fresh injection of S$1.2 billion in mezzanine financing from banks and a property developer from Hong Kong. It solved an immediate funding crisis, but the loveless threesome clung on, with each desperately trying to find new partners to take over the union. By 2010, three years after the consortium first won the tender, construction still had not begun. Any further delay would bust the deadline of 2016, which URA had imposed for the project to be completed.

Finally in 2011, Dubai World found a buyer for its stake and the S$155 million price was acceptable to CDL to exercise its first right on the one-third equity stake in the joint venture. El-Ad also found a new buyer in Malaysia-based conglomerate IOI Corporation, a global leading palm oil player. Then, CDL and IOI restructured their interests to allow IOI to raise its stake to 49.9 per cent. CDL would hold a majority stake in the consortium with 50.1 per cent. Both sides pumped in fresh funds to redeem the mezzanine notes. The long torment finally came to an end and construction began in 2011.

Behind closed doors though, teething problems came to the fore between CDL and IOI. The Malaysian side wanted parity and pushed the Singaporeans to sell the 0.1 per cent to them. But Kwek, having been burnt by the Arab-Israeli tag team, refused. "He wanted control," said Chia. "Chairman was insistent not to give. Both sides couldn't agree during meetings and then we had already arranged for lunch after that. Oh, the lunches were so tense. No one was talking and we had to eat in silence. So awkward! I dared not even cut the meat!"

But operationally, Kwek gave instructions to treat IOI as equal partners and consult the Malaysians on all major decisions. It worked out eventually, and the project was completed in 2016, just months shy of the official deadline. The end result was a proud urban oasis, with an abundance of space unlike most compact downtown developments. Flanked by its short neighbours Raffles Hotel and Suntec City, The South Beach looks absurdly statuesque and eye-catching. An alien-like arrival that somehow manages to exist coherently and glamorously with its surroundings.

It has since lived up to its promise of a green building, winning the ASEAN Energy Awards in 2019 and the top Green Mark Platinum certification in Singapore. In 2021, URA also gave The South Beach the Architectural Heritage Awards for its conservation efforts. The nine-year nightmare had found a sweet ending, and Hong Leong and Kwek were finally back in Beach Road. It is a fitting monument to the memory of his father, the founder of the company. There would not be such a pleasant denouement with his next dramatic challenge.

Part 6

Feeding Solutions, Starving Problems

"

You need aggressive people who are solution-minded and have foresight. Otherwise, you can never grow.

— Kwek Leng Beng

Chapter 18

Yours Sincerely

"A rare moment of public discord is fuelling concerns that the close-knit clan will become distracted at a critical time for its sprawling empire."

— **Bloomberg**, *December 2020.*

While Kwek Leng Beng had expanded his family business into Asia, the United States, Europe, New Zealand, and even the Middle East, there remained a glaring omission in his global conquest — China. The challenge of breaking into the world's biggest market would be given to his son Sherman. In 2010, the third-generation Kwek started CDL China with an aim to replicate City Developments Limited's (CDL) Singapore real estate success in the world's second largest economy. It was a big job, especially given the family business' lack of success in the country. In many ways, China had long been somewhat of a thorny challenge for the Kweks.

In the mid-1990s, as the People's Republic embarked on renewed reforms after the Tiananmen Incident, Hong Leong engaged the consultancy of Singapore's former Deputy Prime Minister Goh Keng

Swee to go into hotels in China. Goh was an adviser to the Chinese government in its reform and opening up policy. Progress was slow.

At about the same time, Hong Leong also acquired famous Chinese electrical appliance brand Xinfei Electric, which was a household brand in China for its refrigerators. Xinfei came under Hong Leong Asia, the trade and industry arm of the Hong Leong Group. But by 2018, Xinfei went bankrupt and Hong Leong Asia suffered a loss of S$43.5 million. Observer Jack Xu wrote on *Weixin* in December 2020: "Investing in Xinfei turned into Hong Leong Group's 'Battle of Waterloo' in China." He spoke too soon. There was a bigger battle on the horizon.

Amid a deal which had all the hallmarks of a game-changer for CDL, it ultimately became a disaster amid geopolitics and a pandemic that spiralled out of control. While Kwek Leng Beng had skipped through crises repeatedly with an unshakeable confidence that became a hallmark of his legend in the business world, he would find the triple whammy of the COVID-19, a partner's meltdown and family problems a challenge almost too much to bear.

His Waterloo moment began when Sherman Kwek tried to expand CDL China. He found the pace much slower than expected. The group was growing at an average of a project a year. "We were late to enter the China market and only set up CDL China in 2010," he said. "We were growing very slowly there and my belief has always been that if you can't achieve scale in a particular market segment or geography, then you will never be a major player or build any economies of scale. Without scale, even hiring people is immensely challenging. Nobody really knew CDL in China."

In 2018, he found a way to catapult CDL China to among the top developers in the country by taking a stake in Chinese developer Sincere Property Group, which was ranked among the top 100 real estate players. From only three cities, CDL would suddenly be in 20 cities, with a pipeline of development projects in mostly Tier 1 and 2 cities. Sincere had a development land bank of 9.2 million square metres in gross floor area across 64 development projects spanning 18 cities in mainland China.

Kwek Leng Beng shared his son's vision and idea. "It was Sherman's desire to get this platform so that we can extend in China," he said. He was introduced to Sincere founder and leader Wu Xu, and came away impressed. He recalled: "Sherman and I met him and he brought us about Shanghai. We saw the way he operated, his best connections, his business acumen. We were impressed. Put it this way, I knew that what we would do with him would be very impressive."

Like grandfather, like father, like son, the Kweks saw in Sincere a short cut to scale and success in China real estate. Similar to the CDL deal of 1969, the Copthorne acquisition in 1995 and the Regal buy of 1999, Sincere would be the latest in a string of bulk buys that would push Hong Leong and the Kweks into the next stratosphere. Both Kwek Leng Beng and Sherman Kwek even used the same phrase repeatedly to describe these landmark purchases: "With a stroke of a pen, we could..."

In May 2019, CDL said it was taking a 24 per cent stake in Sincere for 5.5 billion yuan, or S$1.1 billion then. It was CDL's single largest investment in China to date. Sherman Kwek said at the media briefing: "This transforms our company especially in China, where it was very painful for us for the last seven to eight years to buy one project at a time...Now we can seriously bulk up on scale and grow with our partner with the necessary expertise on the ground." At the same time, CDL announced that Sherman Kwek was appointed to the board as an executive director, joining his father and his uncle Kwek Leng Peck.

It was going swimmingly for the young Kwek. "Being a Top 100 developer in China, Sincere would have been our key platform of growth there and I had plans to eventually rename it as CDL China," he said. "It would have turned us into a powerhouse in China, just like we are in Singapore. I was buying a platform with a sizable landbank and a big team, and not just a bunch of assets. This is similar to how our group took over CDL when it was still loss-making. Obviously, the key difference is that Sincere was carrying a heavy debt load and needed to be deleveraged and restructured."

As CDL conducted due diligence into Sincere, the Singaporeans discovered that the Chinese firm was in a worse financial state than they had expected. Like most developers in China, Sincere was heavily leveraged. Its net gearing was already at 200 per cent in May 2019, and as China walked into the COVID-19 crisis in early 2020, Sincere got more desperate. Its debt load was S$6 billion. Instead of being frightened off, Sherman Kwek saw an opportunity. He wanted to wrest control of Sincere at a better price than what was agreed in 2019. The 2019 deal was not completed as Sincere had not satisfied certain conditions. "I felt that we could save it and turn it around, then China would be one of our biggest markets," he said.

He put forth a package for CDL to acquire 51.01 per cent, more than double the 2019 deal, at a cheaper price of 4.39 billion yuan (S$880 million). It also included a call option that CDL could exercise to buy an additional 9 per cent interest in the firm for 0.77 billion yuan — the same valuation. Together, CDL would then hold a 60.01 per cent stake in the firm for a total of 5.16 billion yuan. In early 2020, this proposal was put to the CDL board for approval. The cracks became evident during the long meeting — about three hours long, shared Sherman Kwek — when various concerned directors debated the issue vigorously. In the eight-person board, with Sherman Kwek choosing to abstain because he had proposed the project, it came down to a narrow vote in favour of acquiring Sincere.

In April 2020, the announcement was made. In a statement to the Singapore Exchange, CDL made clear it was taking advantage of a distressed sale, saying: "Given the adverse impact of the COVID-19 crisis and the global uncertainty, CDL has taken the opportunity to negotiate new terms for its investment into Sincere Property, which are significantly improved over the terms announced last year." Sherman Kwek said it was a "game-changing investment" and that he was very optimistic about the tie-up between CDL and Sincere.

"1+1 can be bigger than 2," he said. But analysts quickly wondered aloud if CDL was "throwing good money after bad" since the deal was delayed and Sincere's steep valuation discount.

Meanwhile, the pandemic had begun to ravage global economies, with CDL's hospitality business severely impacted as borders closed and tourism all but evaporated in a manner the world had not seen in generations. In Singapore, the government announced a "circuit breaker" to effectively send the entire country into a lockdown in the same month. Sherman Kwek had delivered his remarks via a virtual conference.

To make matters worse, CDL was dealt an unforeseen blow by the Chinese authorities. In August 2020, China's financial regulators introduced measures to rein in the highly-indebted developers — the likes of Sincere. In a move widely referred to as the "three red lines," restrictions to cap borrowings by developers were further tightened, effectively making it near impossible for Sincere to turn around its fortunes unless there was a massive injection of funds. By then, there was almost no chance of CDL putting in more money, said director Philip Yeo. "Without the three lines, we could have meandered through," he said. "It reached the point when it was not possible to save Sincere." The CDL board began to waver, with the thin majority about to give way.

Trouble was also brewing behind closed doors within the Kwek clan, whose Hong Leong Group holds a controlling stake in CDL. Several were not in favour of the Sincere deal and wanted to cut their losses, which amounted to S$1.8 billion including investments and loans made to Sincere. Letters were sent to both Kwek Leng Beng and Sherman Kwek, demanding that the Sincere deal did not go through. To force the issue, CDL director Kwek Leng Peck surprised his cousin and nephew by resigning from the board in October 2020.

While relations between them had been strained for months, neither executive chairman Kwek nor CEO Sherman Kwek expected him to quit a position he had held for more than three decades. "We didn't know he was resigning and it came as a shock to everyone," said Sherman Kwek. It did not help that Kwek Leng Peck put in writing that he was leaving because he did not agree with the board on the group's investment in Sincere and its management of its hotel business. This was not a friendly exit. It was hostile.

As expected, it grabbed media attention immediately. *The Business Times* in Singapore called it "one of the most stunning" developments in CDL's history. *Bloomberg* said it was "a rare moment of public discord" in the Kwek family, a dynasty which the Bloomberg Billionaires Index ranked as worth US$16.5 billion in 2020. Cecilia Kwek, the wife of Kwek Leng Beng and mother of Sherman Kwek, did not mince her words in her first public comments on the incident. "It hurt my husband, it hurt my elder son, it hurt me. It was a big let-down," she said. "They did not hold our hands."

The split brought into the open decades of disquiet within the Kwek clan which is mainly divided between businesses in Singapore and Malaysia, linked at the top by familial ties across four branches led by Kwek Leng Beng's father Kwek Hong Png and his three brothers, all deceased. While the markets on both sides of the Causeway had long spoken of tensions and factions in the clan since the 1990s, the dynasty had been able to keep a lid on differences bubbling to the surface.

Unlike the feuding Ambanis in India and the Hos in Macau, where tussles are fierce and public, the Kweks had succeeded in maintaining relations on an even keel, said Kwek Leng Beng's nephew Kwek Eik Sheng. "Every family has their own problems. Our family is no different," he shared. "But it's always been very private. Any unhappiness, we discuss it privately. So this is the first time it came out in public." Several long-serving Hong Leong staff who have interacted with various members of the clan over decades all described relations as "cordial" in interviews for this book. Cecilia Kwek said that the relatives visit each other during Chinese New Year and the wives remain in regular contact.

As the pressure within the clan built to a crescendo, two other directors who were not in favour of the Sincere project also joined him, resigning in the next few months. The departures rocked CDL and the Singapore market, said observers. "This focused the market's attention on Sincere Property Group's troubles, and sparked a sell-off in CDL's shares," wrote a commentator in *The Business Times*.

By early 2021, after financial advisors Deloitte & Touche conducted a review into Sincere, Kwek Leng Beng decided to jettison the deal by writing off almost all of CDL's S$1.8 billion investment in the Chinese firm. It meant a full-year net loss of S$1.92 billion for the company in 2020, compared to a profit of S$564.6 million the previous year. It was CDL's first full-year loss since the early 1970s. Kwek said that while he had high hopes for Sincere, the deal did not work out. "Little did I know that his wavelength and our wavelength are different," he said, referring to Wu Xu. "We would realise later that his way of doing things is not the way we would like."

It was a major blow to Sherman Kwek, who believed that CDL could have helped Sincere reverse its fortunes in a post-pandemic China. "I suffered much reputational damage from this failed investment and I've come away with many deep bruises," he said. "It was the darkest and most painful period of my career. Nonetheless, I have also learnt many lessons from this episode and will tread more carefully in the future." Kwek Leng Beng said his son had to learn this hard and difficult lesson, learn due diligence, and importantly, he must learn to move on. The patriarch stressed the futility of dwelling on the loss. "We should not keep talking about Sincere... we must now forget about all these old subjects...we must look forward," he said at CDL's results briefing in February 2021.

CDL and Sincere would enter a brief and public war of words in the next few months, as Sincere tottered towards bankruptcy. In March 2021, it missed a deadline to repay the principal on a bond that matured, reported *Bloomberg*. Three months later, Sincere was sued for bankruptcy in a Chinese court. In September 2021, Kwek

Leng Beng decided to cut all ties with Sincere. He exited the ill-fated investment for US$1, selling its stake in the Chinese company to an unrelated third party incorporated in the Republic of Seychelles.

He said: "I'm a very decisive man. I decide, cut loose, finish. Let's move on. Don't be burdened every day, worried. For what? And you have to cut loose. Then you can go on and do well. It's okay. I saw this quote online the other day and I liked it a lot — 'Effective people are not problem-minded. They are solution-minded. They feed solutions and starve problems.' In other words, when there are problems, let's solve it. Instead of complaining — problem, problem, problem, problem — find a solution. People have since asked me if I can be sure never to make the same mistake again. I tell them, 'How can you say never?' I'm a practical man. In business, you can never say never. But the key is to find solutions when you have a problem."

Philip Yeo agreed that although it was painful, it was the right decision to exit. "Otherwise, it would be worse. If we had not let go in 2021, it was no better in 2022. I still believe we would lose more money if we didn't stop," he said. It was a rare major blemish in Kwek's career, even though the Sincere deal was very much under Sherman Kwek's leadership and management, observed Yeo. "To be fair to the chairman, if not for Sincere, the company has been doing very well," he stressed. "For the company to lose S$1.8 billion and still be around — it's no joke."

Those close to Kwek Leng Beng said that he was visibly affected by the combined strains of the COVID-19 pandemic lockdowns, the Sincere debacle and the family clashes. But the man himself was typically defiant. When asked if Sincere had been the most difficult challenge of his career, he gave a slight smirk and replied: "I don't think so." Fixing the family fissures would take a lot longer. But by early 2021, in the midst of the darkest days of the Sincere episode, few realised that Kwek was already plotting his next business move to rebound in a most spectacular fashion.

Chapter 19

Hwaiting!

"All things came together at the same time."

— Kwek Eik Sheng, group chief operating officer of City Developments.

In the depths of the COVID-19 pandemic and the Sincere saga, Kwek Leng Beng would find an unlikely break. Seemingly from out of nowhere, a Korean buyer approached City Developments (CDL) in August 2020 with an interest to buy the Millennium Hilton Seoul. "It was almost out of the blue, a cold call saying they want to purchase this hotel for over 700 billion won (US$490 million)," said Kwek Eik Sheng, nephew of Kwek Leng Beng and then the group chief strategy officer. The timing could not have been better. Kwek's hotel empire had been savaged by the pandemic, Sincere was plunging deeper into the red and family members were demanding results. It was a chance for Kwek to charge back, or as the Koreans would cheer: "*Hwaiting*!" — Korean English for "fighting" or simply "come on."

Within the company, it was an open secret that the hotel had been an operational nightmare. While it was a trophy hotel which

Kwek proudly snagged in 1999 from Daewoo after the Asian Financial Crisis, it had not exactly been a gleaming property to manage. Since the beginnings, the prized site at the foot of Mount Namsan had been plagued by trouble. The Singaporeans had to take Hilton to court after the hotel chain broke a non-compete clause and opened another Hilton next door. CDL also had a legal tussle with former Daewoo chairman Kim Woo Choong after the former owner no longer visited the penthouse and was subsequently jailed for corruption.

But these problems were minor compared to the massive challenges posed by the hotel's trade union, inherited by CDL from Daewoo, said Patricia Yeo, group finance director in Hong Leong Investment Holdings. "We had a lot of union problems," she shared. "We went through many, many permutations of how to solve the problem. The cost structure was so high because of the union. We just can't make money because there's a limit to how much you can keep raising the hotel room rates if we wanted to stay competitive."

The hotel's staff union strengthened with the entry of its foreign owner, becoming a challenge for the group to manage over the two decades, observed Kwek Eik Sheng. "Challenges from the union were getting worse every year," he said. "They would threaten to strike every year over pay issues. The region was also hit by geopolitical tensions with Japan and China and the profit margins were declining. It was an asset which gave us a lot of headaches." Millennium & Copthorne (M&C) tried to sell the hotel once in

2008 at about 575 billion won, but the deal was scuppered when the buyer, Korean property developer Kangho AMC, defaulted amidst the Global Financial Crisis in 2008.

In 2020, there was another opportunity to let go of this troublesome trophy. It helped that M&C had just been delisted a year earlier, giving the Singapore management freer rein to negotiate the deal. After six months of negotiations, it signed a memorandum of understanding in February 2021 with IGIS Asset Management, one of South Korea's largest real estate managers. The price was for 825 billion won, or about US$580 million, for the hotel and its adjoining plot of land. It was a cool profit from the US$213.5 million paid by Kwek in 1999. Coming at a time of the pandemic and the Sincere incident, it was a win which Kwek desperately needed. The timing was perfect…or so everyone thought.

Not Kwek. He felt he could do better. He believed the hotel was worth more. As it turned out, he was very far from being desperate. In June 2021, he ordered his team to walk away from the deal, revealed Kwek Eik Sheng, who was shocked. "We had spent about a year on it and incurred a big chunk of legal costs. But the chairman believed the deal wasn't that good and that this thing was worth more than a trillion won. We thought it was quite a leap," he said with a weak smile. "Very big jump? Exactly, right? We couldn't even get an independent value from the ground because as a hotel it was only worth a fraction and it was anybody's guess what the right buyer could do with this site and what the value would be." Among other things, Kwek Leng Beng believed that the sale came with conditions which were far from ideal for his company. CDL had to pay the fees to terminate the operator Hilton prematurely, and it also had to compensate the retrenchment of the union workers.

A few weeks after the Singaporeans ended negotiations, the Koreans returned with a higher offer. The new price finally met Kwek's expectations — 1.1 trillion won, or US$845 million. Kwek had nearly quadrupled what he paid 22 years ago, netting about US$400 million in profits, making it the most lucrative project in his career. "It is not easy to achieve record profits," said Kwek Eik Sheng. "He held up, called their bluff and got almost everything we wanted. He believed our site was worth a lot. He may not handle the numbers directly but he believed there were other parties who would buy and that we could wait for a better deal. He was proven right." To top it off, the Koreans agreed to bear the costs to compensate Hilton and the union workers. It was a near slam dunk for the Singapore company. As a senior CDL aide said in near disbelief: "And all these happened in 2021, while the COVID pandemic was still going on." Such profitability is rare in the industry, observed veteran hotelier Daniel Desbaillets, who is an independent director in CDL. "This man is a genius. You give him $1, and like the mystery of a magician, it becomes $3," he said.

The entire Millennium Hilton Seoul episode across more than two decades was illustrative of Kwek Leng Beng's unparalleled understanding of business, said Patricia Yeo. "He was optimistic. So working with him taught me a lot. I don't know how to be as optimistic as he is," she said. "I can say this now because I know how it ended. Because along the way, we were fraught with difficulties operating it. But it never mattered to him. Somehow, he had this ability to just hold out and focus on the big picture. I don't know how he knew there was something else out there!"

Kwek said he has always believed that the Seoul hotel was a tremendous asset, to be unlocked at the right time and at the right price. And it is precisely because of the unpredictability of business that it is pointless, and in fact counter-productive, to belabour and bemoan a loss — even one as huge as Sincere. It is more useful to move on and recover, or in his words be solution-minded. His son Kingston pointed out his dad's laser-like ability to focus on the crux and dismiss the background noise. "My father believes the way the world works is there is usually one master reason behind a course of action, along with one main problem associated with doing it," he said. "In deciding whether to do something or not, it's not deciding between the many reasons for against the many problems, but rather if the one master reason for outweighs the main problem. He narrows down the lines of reasoning into one master reason that can explain everything."

Such distillation offers a simplicity that often eludes many in life and work, especially in an era of information overload and omnichannel possibilities. Kwek Leng Beng said: "That's exactly how we managed to make more than S$1 billion in Korea, which is such a difficult country to operate in," he said. Like an old singer back on tour, he was once again playing the crowd favourites from his top-selling albums of yesteryear — profits, values and dividends for shareholders. Rumours of his demise have been greatly exaggerated, oh ye of little faith. The man was far from ready to be written off, as he did a K-Pop dance at the pinnacle of a business he had long bent to his unyielding will.

His peers were utterly impressed. Far East Organization's CEO Philip Ng let out a "wow" when the Seoul Hilton project was mentioned. "That's a very good deal. It's a big gain. Wow, that's a huge gain from the time that he bought it," he said. "So again, you know, those days people in Singapore would be looking at Hong Kong and maybe China. But South Korea and Japan, all these places were very unfamiliar. And we would hesitate to go because there was a language problem. Laws are different, rules and regulations. He was quite bold, and it turned out well because I think his reading was that the framework may be a little different right now, and so on, but these are places that you can do business."

It is yet another sign of Kwek not only as a doyen of the hotel world but also a champion contrarian, said former Hilton CEO David Michels. "Leng Beng's unique. He has been in the business for more than 50 years. Very few people have been in this industry that long as an owner," he observed. "The brands have been around longer, but never one individual. Hotels go on forever, but most owners go bankrupt. And in the hotel business, you make money from selling and buying, not from operating. But he doesn't sell much and has somehow still prospered."

To top it off, Kwek's hotel business is infamous in the industry for frequent culling of its top executives, creating a revolving-door culture, and yet it somehow works. One of his favourite sayings is: "If I want loyalty, I would get a dog." It was "his quip to summarily dismiss excuses for underperformance," explained his nephew Kevin Hangchi. Michels added: "He has defied every logic of the hotel business: you should sell hotels, you should be able to employ great employees, you should keep people loyal for years. Somehow Leng Beng has done everything you shouldn't do, and he's not only still there, but he's still prosperous. Somehow he manages to balance the whole thing into the world's biggest hotel-owned company. I have witnessed it but I can't explain it. I haven't been jealous of many people but if I'm jealous of one person — it is him because I don't know how he bloody does it. It's extraordinary."

The Seoul deal not only grabbed the attention of the hotel world, but it would also shine a bright end to two years of gloom in CDL and the Kwek family. In December 2021, *The Business Times* of Singapore ran a front-page story headlined: "With troubles behind it, CDL can enter 2022 with a spring in its step." It added in the article: "Investors can be buoyed that CDL has a strong pipeline of development projects in a hot Singapore residential property market and the group is able to successfully recycle capital by divesting assets at juicy premiums to book value."

Eight months later, in August 2022, CDL would prove the projection true, posting a record net profit of S$1.1 billion for the first half of the year, reversing a net loss of S$32.1 million in the same period in 2020. It was the highest net profit achieved by CDL since its creation in 1963. Much of it was due to the gains from the sale of Millennium Hilton Seoul. The good news was further bolstered by the easing of border restrictions and rebound in travel after two years. The group's hotel revenue per available room grew 110.4 per cent, led by the Europe and US markets. "All things came together at the same time," said Kwek Eik Sheng. "The timing was very good. About as good as you can get."

To accompany the news, the newspaper ran a photo of Kwek Leng Beng with CEO Sherman Kwek, COO Kwek Eik Sheng and group general manager Chia Ngiang Hong. The symbolism was not lost on the matriarch of the family, Cecilia Kwek. Her husband, her family, and their company had bounced back. She sent a text message to Chia: "Great, we did it!" The Kwek Leng Beng Inc was back.

CHAPTER 20

Succession

"On paper, it looks like he will be a tough act to follow."

— The Business Times' *Kalpana Rashiwala on Kwek Leng Beng in 2012.*

In the ornate ballroom of Caroline's Mansion, the lush fittings conveyed luxury, importance and impeccable personal prestige. The exclusive venue adjacent to the main St. Regis Singapore evoked the charms of 19th-century New York grandeur, from coffered ceilings to plaster crown mouldings, an exclusive space completely at odds with its bustling Orchard Road address. As a homage to the founding Astor family of St. Regis, which are among the earliest tycoons of the United States, it was fitting as the place where the Kweks would finally gather after some two years of pandemic-enforced restrictions.

In January 2022, amid a strict atmosphere of self-distancing, the family of Kwek Leng Beng and the senior management of City Developments Limited (CDL) and Hong Leong companies would gather for a corporate event and give the patriarch an 81st birthday surprise. Masks were kept on, intermingling between tables were disallowed, but there was an unspoken relief that the family and the business had finally put behind two years of troubles and pain. The pandemic had put paid to a big 80th milestone bash in 2021, but a year late may still be tolerable for the uber-punctual octogenarian who, not surprisingly, arrived 15 minutes early for his own event.

After cutting his cake on stage with his family, a visibly delighted Kwek removed his mask and thanked his son Sherman for organising the party, which included a hilarious deepfake video of former United States President Donald Trump paying tribute to his erstwhile the Plaza Hotel conqueror from Singapore. "I don't mince my words. But I really love all of you very much," he said, offering rare words of tenderness. "You give me the inspiration and desire to do better and better, to pass on to the next generation and guide them to carry on when I retire," he said, before an uncharacteristic punchline. "In another 10 years or so." The crowd laughed.

The issue at heart, though, is no laughing matter. Succession in Hong Leong has been much talked about for decades in public, but with little public input from Kwek Leng Beng and the other members of the family. As CDL is a public listed entity, there has been no lack of interest and even demand from the public, media and shareholders for greater clarity as to who next after the current executive chairman. In 2012, *The Business Times* ran a commentary headlined: "Time for CDL to spell out succession plans." In it, the daily's property correspondent Kalpana Rashiwala urged: "Mr Kwek is 71, and could well continue to helm the group for several more years. However, it would be good if CDL discloses the designated successor to Mr Kwek, as investors would prefer to have greater certainty about the group's future leadership."

Ten years later and after the COVID-19 pandemic, as Kwek moves into his 80s and amid a family fallout as a result of the Sincere incident, the question of succession takes on greater urgency. The answer of course lies in Hong Leong and the extended Kwek clan. Since Hong Leong Group is the biggest shareholder of CDL with 48.55 per cent, he who controls Hong Leong will in effect lead CDL. As Rashiwala observed in 2012: "It would be a fair guess that Mr Kwek's successor would be a family member." After all, the best predictor of future behaviour is past behaviour. Hong Leong has kept it in the family and done a very good job at that.

Founder Kwek Hong Png always meant for Hong Leong to be a family business and to remain so. He had his sights on his elder son Kwek Leng Beng as his successor since the early days of his business. "We did expect Leng Beng to take over," said Kwek Geok Luan, the elder sister of Kwek Leng Beng. "My father had been grooming him since young." Since joining the business in 1963, the young Kwek was gradually exposed to all the different arms of the Hong Leong business, from building materials to finance, from hospitality to property. And bit by bit, the patriarch allowed his son to take over his leadership roles. The first came in 1984, when Kwek Leng Beng succeeded his father as chairman of Hong Leong Finance. The time had come for him "to effect a smooth transition of leadership from the old to the new," said Kwek Hong Png then.

The handover accelerated in 1990 when Kwek senior was barred from holding directorships, after pleading guilty to a charge of not discharging duties diligently and fined S$5,000. It led to Kwek Leng Beng taking over from his father as chairman of CDL and other companies. By the time Kwek Hong Png died four years later in 1994, his chosen successor had already been in the business for more than 30 years, and leading parts of the conglomerate for a decade. Not only was Kwek Leng Beng familiar with all parts of the business, but the market also viewed him as a well-established leader.

So despite murmurings in the Singapore media of challenges from the extended Kwek clan to Kwek Leng Beng as the new boss, the rumours turned out to be wide off the mark. A day after Kwek Hong Png passed away, *The Business Times* reported of a family meeting among cousins to discuss who should head operations. The family vehemently denied such a meeting. In an interview for this book, Kwek Leng Beng said that there were no disputes in 1994. "No, there were no challenges from my cousins," he said. "They had no objections."

It led top Singapore retired politicians to praise the Kwek succession publicly. Former Deputy Prime Minister Goh Keng Swee, who was a consultant to the Hong Leong Group, said the way the business had been handled by the second generation of the Kwek family had been "very well done." He was joined by another founding

Old Guard leader Ong Pang Boon, a Hong Leong director, who said that "there exists a good degree of co-operation between the two groups," referring to the operations in Singapore and Malaysia.

Company observers were just as glowing in their feedback of the succession. "Although the patriarch was consulted on all the big business moves, he delegated most of the decision-making to elder son Leng Beng and his team of professional managers who, under the father's tutelage over the years, understood how he made decisions — which were basically very bottom-line oriented," said Yamaichi Merchant Bank analyst Alan Cheong in *The Straits Times*. An unnamed analyst with a foreign broking house told the paper that there would be no problem with Hong Leong's succession. "He has already set in place the foundation on which his later generations will carry on. His sons Kwek Leng Beng and Kwek Leng Joo are already well-established in their own right and they have been more hands-on with the business now than their father." The market confidence in Kwek Leng Beng as the new boss was reflected in the local bourse, with share prices of Hong Leong Group's companies largely moving up.

The fortunes of the group in the 1990s and the new millennium would confirm such post-Kwek Hong Png optimism, as Kwek Leng Beng led the family business from a largely Singapore-centric outfit into a global player with trophy hotels. Along the way, and pretty early on, it seemed clear that Kwek Leng Beng would stick to his father's succession playbook. In other words, keep it in the family, bring in the siblings and groom the next generation into the business early to create a long runway before he hands over. He had a major setback in 2015 when his brother Leng Joo died from a heart attack, depriving him of an experienced lieutenant. "It was tough on Leng Beng because he was all alone," said former top Singapore civil servant Philip Yeo. "Sherman was still young."

When his elder son Sherman Kwek graduated from Boston University and completed his mandatory military service in Singapore in 2000, Kwek Leng Beng wanted him to join the family business right away. But Sherman Kwek demurred, preferring to obtain external work experience elsewhere. "My father was not pleased as he felt that I could learn more and gain greater exposure within a family-run business, but thankfully he also didn't stop me," said Sherman Kwek. "I did give him my assurance that I would come back one day."

The young Kwek worked for two years in venture capital and investment banking in New York. But after the September 11 tragedies in 2001, and the severe impact on CDL's hotel business, Kwek Leng Beng spotted an opening to convince his son to join the business. He asked his Millennium & Copthorne's (M&C) top man in the United States to reach out to Sherman Kwek. "He asked me to consider joining the M&C hotel operations in the US and help out during such critical times," recalled Sherman Kwek. "It was then that I felt the call of the family." In 2002, he started work in M&C in New York as a management trainee, joining three older cousins who were already in the business — Patricia Yeo, Vincent Yeo and Kevin Hangchi. The 3G Kwek team would be further beefed up later by Kwek Eik Sheng, son of Kwek Leng Joo. Sherman Kwek's younger brother, Kingston, is not in the business. The second leg of the Kwek succession story had begun.

Over more than two decades, Kwek Leng Beng would put Sherman Kwek through a similar rotation through the family business that he himself went through in the 1960s and 1970s, including setting up CDL China in 2010 to move the company decisively into the world's biggest market. In 2016, Sherman Kwek was promoted to deputy CEO in CDL, assisting then CEO Grant Kelley. Two years later, Sherman Kwek took over as CEO, and was instrumental in privatising M&C in 2019, a move which allowed the group full control and flexibility over its assets. This subsequently led to the sale of Millennium Hilton Seoul and the collective sale of Tanglin Shopping Centre. The delisting from the London Stock Exchange was long desired by Kwek Leng Beng. In the eyes of many, Sherman Kwek's path to take over from his father was on track. But in Sherman Kwek's eyes, it has never been a given. "My father has never said to me that I would be his successor, and when asked by the media over the decades, he had chosen not to respond," he said. "Therefore, it's something I have never taken for granted or automatically assumed."

When asked directly who his successor will be during an interview for this book, Kwek Leng Beng revealed for the first time:

"I nominate Sherman." He added: "He knows everything but he still needs to be polished. His diamond needs polishing. The Sincere saga probably gave him a little bit of a shock. So, he needs time, and I will give him time." Of course, as his words suggest, the choice of a successor is not a decision that Kwek Leng Beng can make on his own. While he can put forth his candidate, it is at best a nomination. The decision on the next leader of the Hong Leong group of companies must be made with the consensus and support of the other branches of the Kwek clan.

The background on relations within the dynasty is thus important. When Kwek Hong Png decided to venture into Malaysia in 1963, he sent his son and his nephew Quek Leng Chan. When Singapore separated from Malaysia two years later, it was decided that Quek would take up Malaysian citizenship and oversee the business across the Causeway. Kwek Leng Beng returned to Singapore. In his autobiography, Kwek Hong Png wrote: "I have placed members of the second generation including my nephews in various executive positions." The idea was to build a unified business empire across the four branches of the first-generation Kwek brothers.

But relations between the different families began to splinter fairly early on, with the main cleavage emerging between Kwek Hong Png and his nephew Quek Leng Chan. News reports in Singapore said that it was because Quek wanted more control of the Malaysian operations. In 1973, Hong Leong's operations in Malaysia became a completely independent entity under the control of Quek.

However, the two Hong Leongs remained linked by complicated cross-shareholdings and of course blood ties.

When Quek moved into Singapore with its acquisition of First Capital Corp in the late 1970s, relations became even more awkward, said the media. In 1993, an unnamed senior banker told *The Straits Times*: "That was viewed as hostile by his relatives because he was encroaching into their territory." Kwek Leng Beng told *The Straits Times* in an interview in 1997 that there was no rivalry between him and his cousin. He said: "Leng Chan had a disagreement with my old man. But I was neutral. It was not personal."

He maintained in an interview for this book that he has no problems with Quek moving into Singapore with his main vehicle which has since been renamed GuocoLand Limited. "I have no objection when my cousin in Malaysia started to come to Singapore," he said. "Malaysia is difficult to do business. So he comes to Singapore. He built the Guoco Tower. Now all his investments are multiplying everywhere. He's become a big investor, big property developer in Singapore. If he doesn't come in, somebody else would come in — it's the same. My philosophy is better to have a relative who comes in, and you coexist with him, rather than an enemy who comes in to fight with you. We coexist openly. There's no quarrel; we respect each other."

Ties between other branches of the Kwek clan remained largely cordial and peaceful over the years, with the odd disagreements and disputes mostly kept under wraps and behind closed doors. The

Sincere incident and Kwek Leng Peck's resignation from CDL's board in 2020 tossed family differences out into the open for the first time. "Even up till today, we coexist," said Kwek Leng Beng. "He needs my signature in his company, I will sign. We need his signature in our company, he will sign. So, you know, there is coexistence." While he was close to cousins Quek Leng Chan and Quek Leng Chye growing up, he said they have drifted apart after they started working.

For now, succession does not require urgent attention as long as Kwek Leng Beng remains healthy. Contrary to reports in *The Business Times* in 2020 speculating that his cousins may remove him in the wake of the Sincere loss, he has remained firmly in position. He has also made clear on more than one occasion that he is not in favour of retirement. Unlike the Japanese Emperor Akihito whom he wanted to do business with, Kwek is not prepared to abdicate. "I love working," he said during a company results briefing in 2011. "I would like to work as long as possible; if not, I can become an adviser because of my years of experience — if my mind is sound." And as he shared during his 81st birthday in 2022, he believed — albeit half-jokingly — he still has a good decade to go.

Of course, he has slowed down as he moved into his 80s. Those close to him noticed a discernible mellowing during the two years of COVID-19 pandemic restrictions. He no longer walked at a breakneck pace, preferring deliberate steps to avoid falls and injuries. But he does early morning walks and *qigong* exercises almost daily, usually by the Singapore River, Botanic Gardens or Robertson Quay.

He even resumed playing tennis during the pandemic and now spars with a coach thrice weekly.

He has long cut down his trips to the United States because it has become harder for him to recover from jetlag. But regular flights to London remained, with each trip as long as a month so that he could slowly savour the delights of his favourite city. In late 2022, he surprised his employees in the United Kingdom capital when he went behind the wheels of his favourite Aston Martin DB9 Volante and drove through the streets of London. "Why not?" he rebutted when his staff raised doubts. He also tested a Tesla and was tickled by its feature which let out a loud farting sound.

He has always been careful with his diet, yet dines out daily — usually Japanese cuisine — because his domestic helper "can't cook." However, even as he cuts sugar and salt, he has not slashed stress from work. Good stress, as he would say, because work is his life and passion. During a visit to Taiwan over Lunar New Year in 2023, he insisted on visiting different hotels daily. This is a man who is strictly business after all.

Still, when the time comes for him to exit the scene, he stressed, the successor must be based on merit more than blood ties. While Sherman Kwek is his preferred choice, he said: "To me, the priority must be for the company to continue to grow. So you need aggressive people who are solution-minded and have foresight. Otherwise, you can never grow. You cannot say that just because he's my son, even if he cannot do the job, let's promote him. That's not my policy. If he's no good and I just put him there, then the whole company will go astray."

He is not against bringing in professionals to run the business, with family members retreating to the background as shareholders — if the family is unable to find or agree on a suitable successor to him. "I am not averse personally to getting an outsider to come and run the company…if my relatives or my son cannot perform," he said in 2011. He added in an interview for this book that he believed that most family businesses have to eventually move beyond the family. "To me, this is a model which I think many family companies eventually have to go on," he said. In many ways, that has already happened in the Hong Leong Group, with the likes of M&C, Hong Leong Asia and Hong Leong Finance managed by non-Kweks for decades.

Regardless of who might take over from him, the successor will have a tough act to follow. Kwek Leng Beng has been one of the most remarkable business success stories of Singapore, transforming a family business into a global conglomerate with footprints across five continents. He has been utterly relentless and ruthlessly focused in consistently delivering results. While many businesses succumbed to an increasingly volatile, uncertain, complex and ambiguous world from the 20th century into the new millennium, he had navigated through crises with insouciance. "He has set such high standards for his successors," said Philip Yeo.

Kwek subscribes to a stubborn predictability in a globalised world of unknown unknowns, based on key fundamentals he learnt from his father. "Land is gold, don't over-borrow, know your subject well, be honest with your partners and be solution-driven," he rattled off towards the end of the last interview for this book. Oh, and of course, be punctual. Or better yet, be early.

He had setbacks, from missing out on Marina Bay Sands to the Sincere incident and even the misfortune of seeing his Millennium Hilton in New York suffer major damage. But as the former CEO of Hilton group David Michels said: "You can't argue with success. He makes mistakes, like everybody does, because it's impossible to be in business without making mistakes." It is an appraisal shared by *The Business Times* in 2012: "Mr Kwek's track record shows far more hits than misses. He's one of the highest-paid CEOs among Singapore property developers but he is also one of the hardest-working head honchos around. An astute industry player, he not only has more than six decades of real estate experience, but is (also) an old hand in the hotels and finance businesses (he helms Hong Leong Finance), not forgetting his experience in trading and manufacturing."

There is no denying that his first love, greatest passion and biggest pride remains the hotel empire he had built. From the humble King's near the Singapore River to the iconic Plaza in New York, he has found remarkable suite success across the world. Asked how he would like to be remembered, he replied: "As the hotel king that brought Singapore around the globe," before adding, "A man you'll never forget." It is an unlikely personal touch for a man who has been strictly business.

Acknowledgements

I am most grateful to Mr Kwek Leng Beng for agreeing to walk this journey with me. He is not the most at ease when being interviewed and often displayed an impatience with questions that drilled into the details. But he never lost his composure and gamely soldiered on politely despite my at-times invasive questions. This equanimity was mirrored by Mrs Cecilia Kwek and Mr Sherman Kwek, who both met me on several occasions to share unvarnished views of her husband and his father, respectively. I am deeply appreciative that they allowed me into their private spaces and thoughts, which often included some of their lives' most challenging and uncomfortable moments.

Through the more than 30 interviews, I was ably supported by the Hong Leong Group's corporate affairs team. Special mention must go to their head and leader Gerry De Silva, who offered me invaluable advice from the starting point to the finishing line. Gerry and I were both alumni of *The Straits Times*, and we bonded easily over our shared newsroom language and culture. His strong deputies Louisa Cheong and Crystal Chan shepherded this book gently and expertly.

This is the fifth book I am working on with publisher World Scientific. The only reason is because I have enjoyed working with the good team led by Max Phua and Chua Hong Koon. Thanks to Jiang Yulin, Nicole Ong, and Jimmy Low for putting the final touches to the book, and to Khoo Yee Hong and Lee Hooi Yean for their marketing efforts.

I had asked designer Truong Quoc Huy for a luxe modern cover which I felt would best capture the design sensibilities of Mr Kwek Leng Beng. This is the fourth book cover we have worked together on, and as always, Huy does not disappoint. I like the elegance which he has always projected on his artwork.

As always, I am deeply indebted to my colleagues at The Nutgraf. I was joined by Aaron Low and Jacqueline Woo during my interviews with Mr Kwek. Jaime Niam helped me sift through the old photographs and painstakingly curate them, while Pearl Lee worked with Huy on the cover design. Clifford Lee took the photographs of our final interview with Mr Kwek in his penthouse office at Republic Plaza. Writing a book can be a very lonely process and I am very glad that I have a solid and dependable team to count on.

Finally, I have to give thanks to my family. My parents, my in-laws, my sisters and their families are always my most ardent supporters and most honest critics. They keep my feet firmly on the ground even as they cheer me on to the next higher level. Of course, I seek to keep improving my craft and in that, I can always lean on my wife Sue-Ann who walks every step with me — often a tad slower, but she would say that is because she has got my back. I would not have it any other way.

Index